AF560316

SCIENTIFIC ATTITUDE

vis–a–vis

SCIENTIFIC APTITUDE

SCIENTIFIC ATTITUDE
vis–a–vis
SCIENTIFIC APTITUDE

DIGUMARTI BHASKARA RAO,
Ph.D.
R.V.R. COLLEGE OF EDUCATION
GUNTUR–522 006
ANDHRA PRADESH
INDIA

Editor
PROF. MARLOW EDIGER,
Ph. D.
DEPARTMENT OF EDUCATION
NORTH-EAST MISSOURIE STATE UNIVERSITY
KIRKSVILLE
UNITED STATES OF AMERICA

DISCOVERY PUBLISHING HOUSE
NEW DELHI—110 002

Reprinted - 2016

ISBN: 978-81-7141-308-9

Scientific Attitude Vis-a-Vis Scientific Aptitude

Published by:
DISCOVERY PUBLISHING HOUSE PVT. LTD.
4383/4B, Ansari Road, Darya Ganj
New Delhi-110 002 (India)
Phone: +91-11-23279245, 43596064-65
Fax: +91-11-23253475
E-mail: discoverypublishinghouse@gmail.com
sales@discoverypublishinggroup.com
web: www.discoverypublishinggroup.com

Printed at:
Infinity Imaging Systems
Delhi

Preface

Scientific attitude is one of the important outcomes of science education and it makes man a reasonable one and keeps him ahead of others in society. Scientific aptitude is a potentiality of future accomplishment in science and it is useful in selecting a career. Both of these, scientific attitude and scientific aptitude, will enhance the ability of mankind to become a successful one. Many studies indicate that one is influenced by the other and both of them help achieve well.

The present research study is intended to identify the level of scientific attitude and scientific aptitude of secondary school students. Six hundred students were made subjects and the standardised tools revealed the possession of these two by the sample. The sample was possessing an average level of scientific attitude and scientific aptitude. Both were having a significant positive interrelationship.

The teacher and taught have to work hand in hand to improve the status of scientific attitude and scientific aptitude as these two have a great influence on human life. Let us hope that the future generations will come up to the expected levels of scientific attitude and scientific aptitude.

Dr. Marlow Ediger **Dr. D. Bhaskara Rao**

Contents

1 Introduction

We are living in a society which is completely drawn into the scientific environment. Science has become an integral part of our life and living. Now, we can not think a world without science. The wonderful achievements of science have glorified the modern world and transformed the modern civilization into a scientific civilization.

Science is no longer confined to a few seriously devoted persons. Since life in the present world invariably warrants, to variable degrees, knowledge of scientific facts and laws, science has now become everyday science for everybody. Teaching of everyday science for everybody has become an unavoidable part of general education. Nobody questions its inclusion as a subject in the school curriculum. It is included in a school's curriculum for the same reasons as any other subject, but in addition science inculcates certain special values peculiar to it and which no other subject can provide. But besides satisfying the usual needs for its inclusion as a subject in the curriculum such as intellectual, cultural, moral, aesthetic, utilitarian as well as vocational values—science learning provides training in scientific method and also helps to develop a scientific attitude of mind in the learner. The qualities imbibed by the learner through learning science are of great value to a citizen living in the society. Hence, science is now made a compulsory subject in every system of school education right from the elementary stage.

Science teaching in schools can make a difference in the lives of children and the difference should be on the positive side of the educational ladder. Much has been said about the importance of children's understanding the nature of the scientific enterprise. This is important for several reasons. In a free society, scientific advancement is dependent upon the will of the people, their will as decision- making citizens to support it and their will as individuals to become scientists. Therefore, liberally educated people in a free society should understand the nature of the scientific enterprise, the social, economic and political factors that effect its development and the personal satisfactions that come to one who pursues a career in it.

Science has been referred to as a self-corrective process of finding out. Or as Niels Bohr expressed it, 'science includes the methods by which man puts limiting values on his pre-conceptions'. Or as Percy Bridgeman expressed it, 'the methods of science consist of doing your demands to get the answer with no holds barred'. Regardless of whether we refer to them as the methods of science, as problem solving, as inquiry or as discovery, there are processes of investigation in science that have been found to be effective in advancing our understanding of natural phenomena. Elements of the process have been defined in various ways and research has clearly indicated that pupils can be taught how to perform them in conducting their own investigations. Furthermore, as they learn to perform the process, they become more independent or self directive in their learning. To become independent in these ways meets a basic need of all children and thus represents a kind of satisfaction that can be achieved in no other way. If properly taught, science can help all children learn how to learn.

Galilio once felt that in questions of science 'the authority of a thousand is not worth the humble reasoning of a single individual.' While learning science, the learner develops certain faculties through reasoning and experimentation which no other subject can provide.

Considering science from the intellectual point of view, it is the most in exhaustible storehouse of knowledge. Since Nature is an inexhaustible source of knowledge, science as a subject, offers the widest range of knowledge to the learners. It has exposed mankind to infinite avenues of knowledge in nature, living and non-living, about the world we perceive and also about the world beyond human perception and thereby it makes us conscious of the unknown to be explored.

Science, besides satisfying the intellectual curiosity of man and providing materials and media for intellectual exercise, has disciplinary effect on the minds of individuals. Since science covers that widest range of knowledge, the learner wonders at the intricacies and mysteries of the Universe, the known and the unknown. These tend to create a broader outlook in the life of the learner.

Further, science is universal in character; it has no barrier of any kind. The scientific revolution began in Western Europe where modern science was born but its home is now the whole world. The fruits of scientific discoveries in one country are enjoyed by the people all over the world. Science is neither concerned with caste, creed or colour nor recognizes territorial barriers. Such a pattern inherent in science will definitely have an impact on the minds of the learners and is expected to help to develop broad-mindedness in them.

The study of science has several other disciplinary values. For instance, science is an interest-awakening subject; its pursuit demands persistent efforts, diligence and patience. Any experimentation in science requires keen observation, concentration of mind as well as accurate representation of facts. There is no place for prejudice or bias in science. Scientific pursuits warrant objective observation and impartial judgement. Engagement in any scientific activity, be it theoretical or experimental, therefore, presupposes intellectual honesty, perseverance, concentration of mind and broad-mindedness. In science we do not conclude or predict any thing on the basis of superstition, traditional belief or hearsay, unless the facts are based on proof. In science there is no place for sentiment or emotion except rationality. A scientific result to be acceptable must be valid for all cases.

In pursuing a scientific problem, one has to define the problem, plan the process, collect relevant data, formulate necessary hypothesis, repeat the processes if necessary, apply to specific cases before generalizing. During this process, one has to be logical and objective at every step. Thus, scientific pursuits demand such qualities as minute observation, scientific attitude of mind, persistence, perseverance, concentration of mind, accuracy of measurement, patience; logical, objective and unprejudiced judgement; respect for other's opinions, respect for truth, etc. These disciplinary qualities of mind, if cultivated through the teaching of science, may be carried over to manifest in the general behaviour of the learner. This will prove useful for living as an efficient social individual in the society. No other subject provides opportunities for inculcation of so many disciplinary qualities of the mind of the learners.

It is hardly necessary to elaborate the utilitarian or practical values of science. The present world is a world of science and technology. Every think or every event happening around us demands some knowledge of simple scientific facts or principles. Without the elementary knowledge and information of science, we will be at a loss. Science is now everyday science for everybody; its knowledge must no longer be confined to the classes but must reach the masses. The achievements and the benefits of science touch all sectors and all levels of the modern society. The modern man has applied science and technology for the well-being of mankind by inventing machines and by harnessing the resources of nature. The gifts of science have been profitably used for making life comfortable and raising the standard of living. But the use of abuse of the wonderful gifts of science depends on man and his mind. The recent advances in the field of science and technology and the wide application of the achievements of science in industry, agriculture, medicine, transport and communication as well as their uses in domestic life justify, more than ever, the utilitarian values of science.

Science has opened innumerable avenues for pursuing different vocations. A student of science can study engineering and technology, medicine, agriculture or any similar subject and make his career in that profession. In addition, scientific activities have given rise to may varieties of crafts and allied services. Science, therefore, gives opportunities for career-making, pursuing professions and vocations. In fact, if we refer to preparation of the individual for the future as one of the aims of education, then science, as a subject, is rightly serving this purpose. In this age of science and technology there is a demand for technical personnel. The maintenance and creation of new departments, new establishments need the services of engineers, scientists and technicians and there will always be need for research workers in new fields of science. Educationist Paul Fredman once said, science is no longer the preserve of a few completely-perhaps abnormally devoted men; it is becoming and increasingly will become, one of the major professions open to any young man of ability, demanding no more in the way of special bent or devotion than medicine or law. But like those other professions, it too will continue to offer a life with characteristic flavour; it will have its own professional standards and its own typical type of thinking and will call forth from its practitioners its own loyalties.

Science has made a tremendous impact on the cultural life of the present day society which is a product of science. The thinking, feeling and actions of a modern man are practically guided by the effects of science. There is an involvement of science, direct or indirect, in all works as well as leisure of a modern man. Our habits and attitudes have also been affected by science.

The study of science brings behavioural change in the learner and enriches his character and personality. Science gives opportunity for creative thinking and constructive imagination. Further, science is a subject where ideas can be experimented upon and verified. The learner develops the habits of searching for the truth. These qualities affect the pattern of behaviour of the learner. The significant aspect of science is that what ever the student learns has immediate application in the world around him.

In society, there will always be problems to be solved. One of the very useful outcomes of learning science is the development of problem solving skill. If properly cultivated through the teaching of science, the student can apply this skill to solve problems in his personal or social life.

One of the aims of modern education is to provide means for utilization of leisure especially in the industrialized societies. There is no end to interesting pursuits in science, intellectual or otherwise. Scientific activities provide the best hobbies and pass times for proper utilization of leisure.

At higher levels, arts and science are in noway different. There can be no good piece of art without application of science, and on the other hand there is artistic or aesthetic element in all scientific activities. The great thinkers have always been stressing the need for the unity of science and arts, for they originate from the same root. In the modern civilization, scientific creations glorify arts and aesthetics and science may be said to be the modern substitute for arts in the sense that it is the result of the same kind of creative thought and action which have generated arts. Plato (427-347B.C.) stated in long before the evolution of modern science, "We have certain tendency, on the part of literary and scientific forms, to diverge and develop along different lines, with growing hostility, which suggest fundamental incompatibility..... this divergence and one-sidedness needs to be overcome. The origin of both literature and science is the same."

Arts and aesthetics are components of culture and civilization. The creation of the universe is a great piece of art. There is aesthetics in the mysteries and harmonies of nature. There is an aesthetic side to the scientist's activities and to his contribution to human culture. On the lowest level he has the satisfaction of adding to the sum of human knowledge; on a higher level he enjoys the subtle pleasure of devising some hypothesis which fits a diversity of facts opening up new areas of knowledge. Appreciation of 'fitness of purpose', the suitability of an apparatus for the job for which it was designed, can give great inward satisfaction. There is a pleasing skill in avoiding or eliminating source of errors and in particular the errors of human observation. Wonder is aroused by neatness with which some material quality or some living activity, can be sorted out from other qualities or activities for examination and demonstration. There is an elegance that runs through the logic and handiwork of the scientists. It is seen in the formulae of mathematicians, it is equally seen in the experiments and observations of great naturalists. The very simplicity of great generalizations of science stirs the imagination. With microscope and telescope the scientist opens up new worlds of wonder and beauty. A speck of living mater becomes a creature of incredible beauty, a snow flake is more lovely than diamonds and a distant star becomes a universe. It is at this level the science shares equally wit the arts; the privilege of contributing to the aesthetic development of the human race.

Culture in addition to knowledge, includes all activities, thoughts, feelings, attitudes, patterns of individual or social life of man. The study of science gives opportunity for the development of favourable traits of human character which become a positive contribution to the cultural life of the society. For instance, with science gaining ground and spreading its influence in the life of man, there has been a profusion of literature based on science. Scientific fiction, being interesting, adds to the cultural heritage of man. Similarly, the literature on history and development of science is no less interesting. It is the study of the origin and development of civilization itself and has developed into a separate branch of study which contributes to the cultural heritage.

The biographies of scientists incorporated in the science course develop a scientific attitude among the learners. The description of the scientists' pursuits, their tenacity and perseverance, etc., are worth reading. Such a study brings out the scientists' attitude towards science and their hopes and frustrations on their way to discovery. Sometimes, even after their invention or discovery, it takes a long time for social acceptance. The facts about the sacrifices of the scientists for the benefit of mankind stir one's imagination. The lives of Galilio, James Watt, Curies and others show how the scientist has to suffer to make an original discovery. The lives of the scientists can inspire the minds of the young learners. It is believed that the study of science and the life of the scientists engender praise worthy humility.

The study of the scientist's way of discovery is more interesting. It gives the learners an opportunity to grasp the essential steps of scientific method or procedure. For example, the story of the discovery of the Laws of Gravity by Sir Issac Newton or the story of the discovery of the cause of malaria by Sir Ronald Ross, will help to make the meaning of science clear. It is useful to give the pupils, the idea how scientists sacrifice their personal comfort for the good of society. Broad-mindedness and selfless service to mankind are the characteristics of their lives.

Science learners can be provided the opportunity for literary expression by being asked to write the details of their observations, procedures and conclusions of scientific experiments they perform. They should be encouraged to write all observations precisely. For example, on completion of a project, an experiment or a field trip or observation of a scientific demonstration, the students may be asked to write an easy describing all aspects of such an undertaking. Here, the student will have to be creative in his writing and will learn the use of right words to describe his experience which is a good exercise in composition and translation of thought and feelings into words.

A scientist is a seeker of truth and scientific facts give a true picture of nature. In scientific pursuits, it requires intellectual honesty at each step. In an experiment, one has to record correct data, collect authentic information and make objective interpretation of observations. Any thing other than truth will lead in wrong results. For exploration of the unknown, scientists have to proceed carefully on the basis of the true picture at each stage of the process. Intellectual honesty and love for truth coupled with sincerity of purpose and virtues are prerequisites in an scientific pursuit. History records that Galilio, even in the face of condemnation and trail of punishment, never lost faith in his conviction because he was convinced of the truth of his observation. It is said that even though he publicly negated his own scientific statement in the trial chamber, he yet muttered outside "oppur si mouve". Bertrand Russell designates this as the voice of the world. Thus, in science, ultimately truth prevails because science is nothing but truth. There can be no better moral value of a subject than this virtue.

Further, science as a subject has three very important virtues peculiar to it. The study of science imparts training in scientific method and develops scientific attitude and scientific aptitude in the learners. These qualities, viz., scientific attitude, scientific aptitude are the major aspects to qualify an individual to live as truly efficient citizen in the present day scientific society.

Scientific attitude is the most important outcome of science teaching. Tough some people view the scientific attitude as the by-product of teaching science, yet a majority of the people consider it as equally important as knowledge aspect. Scientific attitude is a very significant concern of the process of science education. In this connection, the rethinking Science Education (Das, 1989) mentioned the characteristics of scientific attitude as open-mindedness, a desire for accurate knowledge, confidence in procedures for seeking knowledge and the expectation that the solution of the problem will come through the use ofverified knowledge. To develop scientific attitude, the teachers should always remember that without a questioning mind and a spirit of enquiry, studies in science will only mean acceptance of dogma and will never lead to development of scientific attitude in the learners. The students should be made to practice and observe science so that they get the opportunity to feel and develop the components of scientific attitude in their minds.

Scientific aptitude is a potentiality of future accomplishment in science without regard to past training and experience. An individual with right aptitude toward science develops better scientific aptitude which is very useful in selecting a career. Without right aptitude toward a subject one cannot master or show any interest in a subject. Like-wise, without good scientific aptitude an individual does not perform much in science. The presence of certain study skills, persistence factors in learning science and hereditary background are some of the determinants of scientific aptitude. Factors such as physical development, social and emotional maturity, moral character, interests, abilities attitudes may also be considered necessary for the development of scientific aptitude.

Science Education should provide opportunities for the development of scientific attitude and scientific aptitude among the school children. This is the age of attitude and aptitude formation at a high rate.

NEED OF THE STUDY

Objectives proposed for science education always include the development of interests, values, attitudes, aptitudes, and appreciation. Why these are so important and why we should include them in the school curriculum have long been under discussion.

Science educators have long recognized that scientific attitudes are among the most important outcomes, which should result from science teaching. There is a general agreement among the investigators that an individual with scientific attitude looks for natural cause of events; is open-mined toward the work and opinion of others, bases opinions and conclusions of adequate evidence; evaluates techniques and procedures used and information obtained; is curious concerning the things he observes; accurate in observation, experimentation and presentation of data; suspends judgements until accurate information is available; looks for cause and effect relationships; critical including self-criticism; shows intellectual honesty; free from bias and prejudice; averse to superstitions; maintains such ideals as honesty, patience, persistence, fairness and thoroughness.

It has also been realized that without developing scientific attitude, any amount of knowledge in science contributes little to national development and to the process of social change. (Shrivastave, 1983). This is why development of scientific attitude through science lessons has been emphasized by science educators. Unfortunately, this important aspect, scientific attitude, of science teaching has not been studied properly by the research workers.

Hence, it is planned to study the level of scientific attitude possessed by the tenth class students of the secondary schools of Guntur district, Andhra Pradesh.

Along with the scientific attitude, scientific aptitude is another major outcome of science education. Scientific aptitude is concerned with the ability of future accomplishment in science. If an individual is endowed with better scientific aptitude, he will be in a position to pursue science education with which he can climb the ladder of science with ease and effect. It is as necessary as scientific attitude to develop scientific aptitude, and to develop interest in science education.

In India, systematic and sustained research work is lacking in the field of aptitude testing in general and measurement of scientific aptitude in particular (Sharma, 1980). Nevertheless, after the recommendations of the Secondary Education Commission (1952) were adopted, Interest in aptitude testing grew and some independent attempts were made by the Indian researchers to standardize scientific aptitude tests and to study the scientific aptitude of school children. But these studies were mostly carried in northern India and in Kerala, and no such impressive studies were taken up in Andhra Pradesh to study the scientific aptitude of secondary school pupils.

In the present study, it was decided to study the scientific aptitude of secondary school pupils of Guntur District considering the dearth of research work in the field.

In the present study, it was also felt to identify the association between scientific attitude and scientific aptitude as these two are supposed to be having influence on the latter.

OBJECTIVES OF THE STUDY

The following objectives were framed for the present research study.

1. To find out the level of scientific attitude possessed by the secondary school pupils.
2. To find out the level of scientific aptitude possessed by the secondary school pupils.
3. To identify the association between scientific attitude and scientific aptitude at secondary school level.
4. To compare scientific attitude and scientific aptitude of boys and girls studying in secondary schools.
5. To compare scientific attitude and scientific aptitude of pupils studying in private and government secondary schools.
6. To compare scientific attitude and scientific aptitude of secondary school pupils studying in rural and urban areas.
7. To compare scientific attitude and scientific aptitude of pupils studying in Telugu medium and English medium secondary schools.
8. To compare scientific attitude and scientific aptitude of pupils studying in residential and non-residential secondary schools.

SCOPE OF THE STUDY

The present study is mainly meant for the study of the level of possession of scientific attitude and scientific aptitude possessed by secondary school pupils, and the relationship between them.

Scientific attitude is a complex behavioural aspect of science. It has so many characteristics and it can be attributed to as many situations as we discuss in science education. We can use it to study at various educational levels, say primary to post-graduate levels; we can use it to associate with various school subjects and its impact on learning and achievement of the school subjects; we can use it to relate with sex, residence, type of school, teaching and learning situations, physical facilities, and so on. But the present study of scientific attitude is concerned with the secondary school pupils, viz., tenth class pupils of Guntur district. It is also concerned with sex, management of the school, locality of the school, residential or non-residential, and medium of instruction. The attitude items included in the scientific attitude scale are- rationality, curiosity, aversion to superstitions, objectivity of intellectual beliefs, and suspended judgement.

The necessity of finding out the best personnel for war services— right from the fighter pilots to cooks- stimulated the psychologists to derive measures of inherent human potentialities for success in specific jobs. Thus the aptitude was distinguished from intelligence and was considered as the capacity to acquire proficiency with the given amount of training, formal or informal, likewise scientific aptitude is concerned with the proficiency in science. Those who studied scientific aptitude- a complex of interacting hereditary and environmental determinant producing predisposition to science learning-focussed on aspects such as its predictive efficiency, group differences, aptitude treatment, interaction on instruction and the like. It is also known that scientific aptitude begins to germinate by about 12⁺ to 13⁺ and tends to be developed in full form by about 15⁺ to 18⁺. With these aspects in mind, the present study is limited to the study of the scientific aptitude of secondary school pupils who will be in the age group of 14⁺ and 15⁺.

As the scientific attitude and scientific aptitude have much importance in secondary school education, the present study was limited to these three aspects and to find out their inter-relationship. Importance was given to sex, locale of the school, type of management, medium of instruction, and residential or non-residential schools. A detailed study was undertaken to study scientific attitude and scientific aptitude of the secondary school pupils of Guntur district of Andhra Pradesh.

IMPORTANCE OF THE STUDY

Science is playing a major role in the present age to satisfy the needs and desires of the people and it has also became one of the major human activities. The search for truth became the dominant motive in the prosecution of science. It has been pursued for so many centuries and attracted even wider extent of attention of very persisted group of people. Science is valued mostly for its practical advantages though it is also valued for gratified curiosity and as an object of great aesthetic charm. It is very obvious that the bulk of mankind value science for the practical advantages it brings with it.

Science was given, a few decades back, a step-motherly treatment and was considered to be a subject meant for less promising students, the more promising students were encouraged to study the classics and mathematics as being more worthy and suitable subjects. Science has now established its claim to be placed in the school curriculum. It has now been recognized as a compulsory subject right from the Elementary Stage and now one of the core subjects at Secondary and Higher Secondary Stages. It has taken a good many years of active and persistent efforts to reach this position.

Science, in curriculum, provides certain values which are not provided by any other subject. All the school subjects are taught because they provide liberal education, they are part of the equipment and preparation for life which we expect the school to give to its pupils so that they may play their part in the community as intellectual citizens. Science takes its place side by side with other school subjects as an essential element of one's education. It affords a knowledge of certain facts and laws and an insight into methods and data peculiar to the domain of science. However, the inclusion of any subject in the curriculum should satisfy the intellectual, utilitarian, vocational, cultural, moral and aesthetic values. Besides these, the teaching of science imparts training in the 'scientific method' and develops scientific attitude and scientific aptitude, which are very valuable and at the same time are transferable to other situations of life. The scientific attitude and scientific aptitude pay a major role in science education, and in the lives of pupils pursuing science education. Identifying the importance of science education, the Science Policy Resolution (1958) of the government of India stated that 'the dominating feature of the contemporary world is the intense cultivation of science on a large scale and its application to meet the country's requirements.' And science has now become a compulsory subject in school curriculum, and is trying to inculcate scientific attitude and scientific aptitude besides the pupils for leading quality life.

Since the beginning of the second half of the present century, science educators have included the development of scientific attitude among the general aims of science education. Curriculum writers commonly include a number of scientific attitudes as objectives for science syllabus. The 'Science-A Progress Approach II' (SAPA II) project (1975) lists as one of its objectives : Develop values, attitudes, value systems and value judgements criteria not only related to science related experiences but transferable to day-to-day experiences through life. Other examples of these attitudes are like honesty in reporting data, open-mindedness, rationality, and objectivity. These have been perceived to be the attributes of scientists in the professional work, and hence desirable as objectives for school curricula.

Many writers have pointed out that knowledge about scientific facts and skill in the use of scientific methods are of little value if there is no inclusion to use them. The scientific attitude represents the motivation which converts this knowledge and skill into action and refers to a willingness to use scientific procedures and methods. It may best be described as 'an attitude to ideas and information and to particular way of evaluating them', a formulation which distinguishes it from 'an attitude to science or scientists' on the one hand and from 'an ability to carry out scientific procedures' on the other.

The scientific attitude as it appears in the science education literature embodies the adoption of a particular approach to solve problems, to assess ideas and information or to make decisions. Using this approach evidence is collected and evaluated objectively so that the idiosyncratic prejudices of the individual making the judgement do not intrude. No source of relevant information is rejected before it is fully evaluated and all available evidence is carefully weighed before the decision is made. If the evidence is considered to be insufficient, then judgement is suspended until there is enough information to enable decision to be made. No idea, conclusion, decision or solution is accepted just because a particular person makes a claim, but it is treated sceptically and critically until its soundness can be judged according to the weight of evidence which is relevant to it. A person who is willing to follow such procedure (and who regularly does so) if said by science educators to be motivated by the scientific attitude.

For many science educators, the importance of the scientific attitude is so obvious that no argument is required to support its inclusion among those things which a school science course should aim to develop in pupils. The idea is also reinforced by the fact that there has been little, if any, argument against its inclusion among the aims of science education. However, while it may be obvious that the scientific attitude is important in the professional lives of scientists and that students learning about science should also become aware of the motive power which impels scientists in their work, it is not a simple matter to move on to the conclusion that school students, many of whom do not intend to become scientists, should actually be encouraged to adopt this attitude themselves.

Two types of arguments are offered by those who do provide reasons for taking this final step. In the first, it is argued that an effective way of learning about the nature of scientific activity is for the student to act out the role of a scientist in the classroom. In this connection, Link (1967) states that 'Every child-not just those who manifest interest or high motivation must be viewed as a young scientist by the teacher of science.... must experience the mode and the excitement and the frustration of the scientist'. The student who enters the role of scientist most fully be the one that adopts for himself the attitude which also motivates the scientist. In the second type of justification, it is argued that not only does the adoption of the scientific attitude for themselves help students to understand the nature of science and the activities of scientists better but scientific attitude represents desirable personal tributes for all people. The tendency to be accurate, intellectually honest, open-minded, objective, and to demand reliable empirical evidence before making decisions may be most clearly seen in the problem-solving activity of scientists, but they also represent predispositions appropriate for solving problems in everyday life as well. Under the influence of such attitude as these, it is claimed that problems will be approached in a manner which is more likely to lead to successful solutions. Possession of scientific attitude is only the mark of a scientifically minded person, but also the sign of a rational one. These benefits of a scientific education are primarily for the individual, but a number of writers have claimed additional benefits for the society. In supporting this, Henry (1947) states that 'As we consider the future responsibilities of citizens, we will probably agree that helping children to become more co-operative, more responsible, more open-minded, and at the same time, more critical minded is certainly worth the effort by adopting scientific attitudes and transferring these to situations in everyday life, pupils can be expected to be more tolerant of other points of view and to be more successful in living and working alongside other people. Behind both these arguments is the assumption that pupils will be benefited by possessing better scientific attitudes both in class room and in the society.

The present study on scientific attitude will reveal the level of scientific attitude possessed by the secondary school pupils which will help to guide the pupils and teachers in taking necessary steps to develop scientific attitude in the pupils.

The second aspect of the present study is what the importance of studying the scientific aptitude of secondary school pupils is? Many researchers indicate that intelligence and aptitudes in specified areas are two important determinants of school attainment and, therefore, are potential predictors of success in all forms of performance in school subject. (Pillai, 1986). The major distinction between aptitude and achievement is temporal- achievement refers to present or past accomplishments; aptitude relates to the possibility of future accomplishment. Achievements depend, in part, on prior aptitudes, and aptitude as a predictor of future achievement involves present and past accomplishment.

For persons untrained in a field, aptitude, either on logical or empirical grounds, may be found to be a complex of intelligence, reading ability, reasoning skill, interests, attitudes, and motor skills. At a more advanced level such as for graduate work in science, achievement in undergraduate courses as determined by grades or tests will become an additional and significant component of aptitude. As these last two sentences imply, attempts to assess aptitude may create a wide array of relevant concepts such as knowledge, intelligence, personality, physique, and motor skill. Achievement on the other hand, refers to tangible accomplishments in the field which in science might be exemplified by knowledge, laboratory skills, or completed research.

The phrase 'scientific aptitude' appears to have a clear meaning until the attempt is made to define it. The simple phrase, then involves a complex of interacting hereditary and environmental determiners which produce the predisposition or abilities spoken of as scientific aptitude. High intelligence is essential to scientific achievement. Additional mental factors that appear to be associated with success in science are intellectual curiosity, ability to apply knowledge to new situations, retentive memory and insight into abstractions. These attributes are similar to those found generally in gifted individuals. Factors such as physical development, social and emotional maturity, moral character, interests, attitudes, and skill may also be the facets of scientific aptitude.

"The scientific aptitude in use implies that persons possessing certain characteristics can be identified and that much individuals can succeed in scientific endevours. Thus, the characteristics of able scientists suggest some of the criteria for locating individuals with aptitude for science. These characteristics include mental acuity, creative abilities, capacity for critical thinking, ability to see relationships, suspended judgement, and open-mindedness. Factors that predispose to such traits constitute at least a part of scientific aptitude" (Henry, 1960).

With the above discussion and definition it is clear that scientific aptitude is involved with many hereditary and environmental factors which are very essential for a successful person. It is also clear that the scientific aptitude predicts achievement of pupils in science and allied subjects. Hence, we can safely say that the study on scientific aptitude of secondary school pupils will trace out the problems concerned with its possession, and ultimately helps in the development of such an important psychological trait.

The identification of association between scientific attitude and scientific aptitude will help in identifying the level of their interdependence. It was expected that there would be a positive relationship between scientific attitude and scientific aptitude of secondary school pupils. Hence an intensive study was also taken up to study the relationship between these aspects in detail.

Some of the major educational implications of the present study are:

1. The scientific attitude, a major objective of science teaching, may be cultivated and developed if found low in secondary school pupils.
2. The scientific aptitude, the predictor of future performance, may be developed to greater extent if found unusual among the secondary school pupils.
3. The study of association between scientific attitude and scientific aptitude may help the science educators for making necessary curriculum decision and in guiding the pupils in proper lines.
4. If there exists any significant positive relationship between scientific attitude and scientific aptitude of secondary school pupils, proper measures can be taken up to promote them.

2

Related Literature

Any worthwhile research study in any field of knowledge requires an adequate familiarity with the work which has already been done in the same area. A summary of the writings of recognized authorities and of previous research provides evidence that the research is familiar with what is already known and what is still unknown and untested. Since effective research is based upon past knowledge, this step helps to eliminate the duplication of what has been done, and provides useful hypotheses and helpful suggestions for significant investigation (Best, 1982).

Citing studies that show substantial agreement and those that seem to present conflicting conclusions helps to sharpen and define understanding of existing knowledge in the problem area, provides a background for the research project, and makes the reader aware of the status of the issue. Parading a long list of annotated studies relating to the problem is ineffective and inappropriate. Only those studies that are plainly relevant, competently executed, and clearly reported should be included.

In searching related literature, the researcher should note certain important elements. They include : 1. Reports of closely related studies that have been investigated, 2. Design of the study, including procedures employed and data-gathering instruments used, 3. Populations that were sampled and sampling methods employed. 4. Variables that were denied, 5. Extraneous variables that could have affected the findings, 6. Faults that could have been avoided, and, 7. Recommendations for further research.

Capitalizing on the reviews of expert researchers can be fruitful in providing helpful ideas and suggestions. While review articles that summarize related studies are useful, they do not provide a satisfactory substitute for an independent research. Even though the review of related literature is not a substitute for an independent work, it is one of the first steps in the research process. It is a valuable guide to define the problem, to recognize its significance, to suggest promising data-gathering devices, to appropriate study design, and sources of data for effective analysis and to arrive at fruitful conclusions.

The search for related literature is a time consuming process, even though it is necessary, as earlier stated, for a good research work. Hence this chapter, Review of Related Literature, is meant for the study of objectives that lead to the inclusion of scientific attitude and scientific aptitude in the school curricula and the level of achievement required in biology to pupils of various courses. It is also meant for the study of the research works related to scientific attitude, scientific aptitude, achievement in biology and the inter-relationship among these three factors of science education.

Education Commission (1964-66) states that 'Science Education must become an integral part of school education; and ultimately some study of science should become a part of all courses in the humanities and social sciences.......The quality of science teaching is to be developed considerably so as to achieve its proper objectives and purposes, viz., to understand basic principles; to develop problem-solving, analytical skills and ability; to apply them to the problems of material environments and social living besides promoting the spirit of enquiry and experimentation. Science strengthens commitments of man to free enquiry and search for truth as its highest duty and obligation. By its emphasis on reason and free enquiry, it even helps to lessen ideological tensions.'

Although science is largely occupied with the understanding of nature at present, its development is tending more and more to help man to understand himself and his place in the world. In such developments, the commission observes that the pursuit of mere material affluence and power would be subordinated to that of higher values and the fulfillment of the needs of individual. This concept of mingling of science and spirituality is of special significance for Indian Education.

It is commonly felt that a child's education cannot be complete unless he has some knowledge of science irrespective of the field of study he wishes to pursue in latter life. Today that great advances in science rendered it absolutely necessary that a fundamental knowledge of science should be the 'sine qua non' of any person who was educated and who wished to lead a life which combined in itself something of scientific aspects of existence.

Teaching is more than the presentation of facts. Teaching is the development of new ways of thinking, a development that reveals itself in increased skills with the problems of life, in new habits of action, in more desirable attitudes and aptitudes, in benefiting personality, and is an improved character. Science can justify its place in the curriculum only when it prejudices important changes in young pupils, change in their ways of thinking, in their habits of action and in the values they assign to what they have and what they do (Hurd, 1954).

OBJECTIVES OF SCIENCE TEACHING

Objectives in any area of curriculum should be regarded as direction of growth and not as ultimate ends to be completely reached. In this respect science is not different from other branches. It is important that objectives should be selected towards which the growth and development of the individual may be directed from a very practical point of view. Objectives need to be selected and stated in such a way that progress towards their attainment may be appraised (Heiss, Obourn and Hoffman, 1950).

A judicious formulation and selection of worthwhile objectives for any school subject goes a long way in enriching and shaping both the teaching and testing in that subject and such objectives should be evolved in relation to the needs of the individual in his society. The 3 main sources for the formulation of the objectives are - (1) the needs and capabilities of the pupil, (2) the specific demand of his social environment, and (3) the nature of the subject matter.

Science teachers have long recognized the need for sound objectives in curriculum planning. In an examination of over 3,000 statements written from 1901 to 1950 by secondary school teachers, Paul Hurd noted that, the objectives of science teaching were the teacher's first consideration in planning curriculum. Objectives strongly influence the organization of the curriculum and at the same time they provide the guide lines on the selection of teaching techniques.

National Society for the Study of Education in its Year book (1947) published the objectives under categories, viz., (1) functional information of habits, (2) functional concepts, (3) functional understanding of principles, (4) instrumental skills, (5) problem solving skills, (6) attitudes, (70 appreciations, and (8) interests.

Bloom, *et al.* (1956) classified the educational objectives into three domains, viz., the cognitive, the affective, and the psychomotor. The cognitive domain includes those objectives which deal with the recall or recognition of knowledge and the development of intellectual abilities and skills. The affective domain includes objectives which describe changes in interest, attitudes and values, and the development of appreciations and adequate adjustment. The work done in that period on manipulative or motor-skill was very less which includes motor activities.

Rai (1963) in his Report on School Science Teaching states that the main objectives for teaching of science should be:

1. To arouse the curiosity of the student about the world we live in and to encourage him to understand the various natural phenomena.
2. To train to acquire the habit of making observation in a planned way.
3. To develop in him scientific attitude.
4. To give him an idea whom a scientist works.

The aims and objectives of teaching general science according to All India Seminar on Teaching of Science (1956) should be:

1. To familiarize the pupil with the world in which he lives and make him understand the impact of science on society so as to enable him to adjust himself to his environment.
2. To acquaint him with the scientific method and enable him to develop scientific attitude.
3. To give the pupil a historical perspective, so that he may understand the evolution of scientific development.

The Directorate of Extension Programmes for Secondary Education, Government of India, in its brochure on 'Evaluation in General Science' sets some of objectives of teaching general science in secondary school as follows:

1. The pupils studying general science should acquire knowledge of the fundamentals of science useful to all in everyday life.
2. They should develop the ability to apply the knowledge in everyday life.
3. They should acquire experimental skills such as : (a) handling apparatus and instruments; (b) arranging apparatus for an experiment; and (c) preserving apparatus, chemicals, specimens, models, etc.
4. They should acquire constructional skills such as : (a) improvising simple instruments and appliances, and (b) repairing certain instruments and appliances of everyday life.
5. They should develop drawing skills such as: (a) drawing and sketching certain objects, instruments and arrangements; and (b) photography in certain objects and specimens.
6. They should be able to locate reliable and recent information from appropriate sources.
7. They should be able to interpret scientific data given in various forms such as tabular, graphical, scientific, etc.
8. They should develop the power of minute observation of their surroundings.
9. They should develop the power of oral expression in science to discuss, argue, describe and raise questions using scientific terminology.
10. They should develop the scientific method in thinking and action.
11. They should adopt the scientific attitude in making statements, accepting information and forming beliefs.
12. They should develop interest in scientific reading and hobbies.
13. They should be able to appreciate the impact of science on life, both personal and social, the struggle through which science has advanced, and the inspiring work of the scientists.

The following similar set of objectives was formulated by the principals of Delhi Higher Secondary Schools in the third summer camp organized by the Extension Department of the Central Institute of

Education, Delhi.

1. To develop in the student a scientific attitude.
2. To develop in the student critical thinking.
3. To enable the student to acquire the fundamentals of scientific method.
4. To develop in the student skill in laboratory techniques.
5. To enable the student to be creative.
6. To develop in the student the ability to apply scientific knowledge and principles to problems of everyday life and new situations.
7. To enable the student to comprehend scientific terms, concepts, symbols, various tables and their uses.
8. To enable the student to construct and interpret graphs, diagrams and models.
9. To enable the student to collect and interpret data for the solution of problems.
10. To enable the student to be familiar with the natural resources of his environment and their uses.
11. To enable the student to be familiar with the trends in modern science.
12. To enable the student to appreciate the beauty and order in nature.

Approach Paper on Science and mathematics in General Education Thought of the possibility of fulfilling the objectives for secondary level for enabling the students to;

a. study a few aspects of physical and life sciences in detail with special emphasis on those areas of concern like food, shelter, health energy, nutrition, and major components of environment;
b. appreciate the need of quantification in the scientific studies;
c. develop in science and ability to put the interest into action;
d. manipulate tools equipment in a proper manner;
e. identify the factors operating in the environment; and
f. collect data, classify and draw reasonable inference.

These above objectives of secondary stage are to be fulfilled along the objectives of primary and middle stages which include- collection of information; classification of objects, events, etc.; identification of cause and effect relationship; development of scientific attitudes; acquainting with natural phenomena; giving emphasis to the relevance of science to daily life; etc.

Bhaskara Rao (1989) states that a teacher must formulate some definite objectives and specifications.... in order to achieve desirable behavioural changes among pupils. He emphasizes on objectives such as knowledge, understanding, application, skill, interest, scientific attitudes and appreciation.

First Asian regional Conference on School Biology held at Manila from December 4-10,1966 recommended the following aims and objectives of school biology teaching in Asia.

1. To develop and instil in student the scientific attitude of inquiry and experimentation.
2. To provide sufficient understanding of the concepts of biology to enable students to become worthy citizens of the world.
3. To develop the opportunities for a practical understanding of the method of biologists which give them confidence to attempt the solution of problems which they have to face in their individual and social lives.
4. To give the student the incentive to pursue the study at higher levels of biology and related fields.
5. To encourage respect and feeling for living things.

National council of Educational Research and Training (Pritam Singh, 1983) put forth the following objectives for biological science.

1. The pupil acquires knowledge of biological terms, concepts, principles, formulae, etc.
2. The pupil understand biological terms, facts, concepts, principles and processes, etc.
3. The pupil applies knowledge of biology in new situations.
4. The pupil develops skill in-

   (a) drawing, (b) manipulating, (c) collecting, (d) dissecting, (e) observing biological specimens, and (f) locating biological information.

5. The pupil develops interest in the living world.
6. The pupil develops scientific attitude towards scientific phenomena.
7. The pupil appreciates the contribution of science to human welfare.

And the latest National Policy on Education _ 1986 states that 'Science Education will be strengthened so as to develop in the child well defined abilities and values such as the spirit of inquiry, creativity, objectivity, the courage to question and an aesthetic sensibility.'

All the above aims and objectives of science stress, directly or indirectly, the importance of scientific attitude, scientific aptitude along with skills, abilities and interests. And also we can sense that a pupil of biology should be in a position to utilize his classroom learning in biology in daily life through proper achievement and application.

SCIENTIFIC ATTITUDE

Science educators have recognized that scientific attitudes are the most important outcomes which should result from science teaching. Much experimentation has been carried on in the field of measuring attitudes and opinions, and most of them have come from the sociologists and the social psychologists. Science teachers and educators are not, however, unaware of the need of some valid and reliable research on the measurements of scientific attitude, its influence on certain school achievements and its development. There is much literature on scientific attitude, but it is concerned only with defining and developing it, not on measuring it in various groups of people. With this it is clear that little was done about the measurement of scientific attitude, particularly at school level.

Shrivastava in his study found that science teachers, non-science teachers science students and non-science students demonstrated positive scientific attitudes.

Bhaskara Rao, Sundara Rao and Mohan Rao (1986) , on the contrary, in their study with experienced secondary school science teachers found that 65 per cent of the sample hold low scientific attitudes. Only 35 per cent of them hold average scientific attitudes and unfortunately no one was with high scientific attitudes.

In another study, Bhaskara Rao, *et al* (1989) found that the prospective science teachers were also holding low scientific attitudes.

The only scientific attitude that was predominant in experienced science teachers was willingness to change opinion to a greater extent. The gradually decreased scientific attitudes were suspended judgement, respect for evidence, critical mindedness, honesty and open-mindedness.

Davis (1935) found that the high school pupils in Wisconsin were not superstitious. The high schools pupils of Wisconsin seemed to have a fairly clear concept of the cause and effect relationship, but they did not seem to be able to recognize the adequacy of a supposed cause to produce the given result.

Caldwell and Lundeen (1931) stated that high school seniors believed slightly more than 20 per cent of a list of superstitions. The high school seniors were apparently affected by about 22 per cent of the superstitious ideas which they were familiar.

In supporting with the study of caldwell and Lundeen, Gopal Krishan (1975) found that the college degree students were not free from superstitions.

Belief in superstitions does not decline with the advancement in grade levels despite the fact that the majority of the 500 pupils belonging to 7,8 and 9th grades were presumably taking or had taken science courses (Keurst, 1939).

Downing (1936) when tested the established conclusion i.e., 'any increased power in critical thought processes or in scientific attitudes develops independently of, or possibly despite, science instruction', found that there was a fairly uniform and gradual increase in abilities from grade, viz., 2500 pupils in grades 8 though 12. Ravindranath (1983) also came to a similar conclusion that there was development of scientific attitude in both controlled and experimental pupils of Class VII over a period of one academic year. The experimental group had developed scientific attitude to a considerable degree in comparison with the controlled group.

Shrivastava in his study obtained the result that the knowledge of science or general exposure to science courses affected the scientific attitudes positively.

According to Gopal Krishna, the graduate students who completely devoted to the science subject only have scientific attitude. So far as specialization was concerned, the students of Zoology, Botany and Chemistry had definite advantage over the other students regarding the development of scientific attitude.

Shrivastava also found that scientific knowledge helped in the formation of scientific attitude.

Contrary to the studies of Shrivastava and gopal Krishna, downing found that the students who had not studied science scored average and high scores on the test of scientific thinking than those who studied science. Gopal Krishna concluded that scientific attitude is not the sole monopoly of science subjects, but is equally capable of being developed among students of non-science subjects also. There was no evidence that science subjects, as they are conveniently taught, have higher powers of scientific thinking. Alpern (1946) also reports that there was no significant relation between the science courses a student had taken and his ability to select sound procedures to test hypotheses. The high school students have not developed the skill as a result of their instruction. Another study of Baumel and Berger revealed that the students who scored high scientific attitude were not necessarily those with high grades in science and the students who scored low were not necessarily those with low grades in science.

Shrivastava, based of his study, stated that scientific attitudes differed in respect of sex in early ages, but no significant difference in male and female teachers revealed and this was due to advancement in age. This was in support of the result of Gopal Krishna.

Bhaskara Rao, Sundara Rao and Mohan Rao and Gopal Krishna found that location, rural and urban, did not influence the possession of scientific attitude.

Science educators have realized the importance of inculcating and developing scientific attitudes among different groups of pupils. Development of scientific attitudes can be achieved only through many directions and associated behavioural factors.

Baumel and Berger (1965) hypothesise that the scientific attitude may be developed with the help of the following factors: (1) Scientific attitudes may be acquired by students at all ability; (2) The science teacher needs to evaluate not only the knowledge achievement of the students but also their growth in scientific attitudes; (3) The student with scientific attitudes will more effectively cope with problems in school and community; (4) Success in developing scientific attitudes depends ultimately on the teacher. The teacher through his actions must be able to convince the students that scientific attitudes are an integral part of his behaviour. His intellectual honesty, willingness to admit error, listening to others' ideas, and dealing with facts in an unbiased way made a favourable and lasting impression upon pupils.

The teachers according to Swarnamma (1987), failed to develop scientific attitude among the pupils of upper primary classes. This was supported by the study of Davis which stated that the teachers of Wisconsin did not consciously attempt to develop the characteristics of scientific attitude. If pupils have acquired these characteristics, they have acquired them by some process of thinking or experiences outside the classroom. So they must try to develop scientific attitudes.

Heiss, Obourn and Hoffman suggest the following methods for the development of scientific attitudes among school pupils: (1) Preservation of democratic procedures; (2) Suggesting projects which give the pupils experience in problem solving; (3) Suggesting problems that require the collecting of evidence of forming conclusion; (4) Stressing frequently the need for adequate data before arriving at a conclusion and that conclusions based on insufficient data should be accepted tentatively; and (5) Dealing with misconceptions most effectively by creating attitudes that will serve as checks on accepting half-truths and superstitions.

Tayler has summarized the findings of the learning studies which reveal the ways in which attitudes are developed. They include: (1) through assimilation from the environment. The things that are assumed by the people round about us, the point of view that is held by our friends and acquaintances; (2) through the emotional effects of certain kind of experiences. In general, if one has had satisfying experiences in a particular connection, he develops an attitude favourable to some content or aspect of that experiences; (3) through traumatic experiences, i.e., experiences that have a deep emotional effect; and (4) through direct intellectual processes. In some instances when we see the implications of particular behaviour, when we analyze the nature of a particular object or process, we are led to develop an attitude favourable or unfavourable to it from the knowledge which we gain from this intellectual analysis.

Tayler further proposes suggestions for planning learning experiences to build desirable attitudes such as : (1) Increase the degree of consistency of the environment; (2) Increase the opportunities for making satisfying adjustments to attitude formation; and (3) Provide opportunity for the analysis of problem situations so that a pupil may understand and then test intellectually in the desirable attitude.

Study of Shrivastave reveals that the amount of scientific knowledge or general exposure to science courses had impact on scientific attitudes positively, and scientific knowledge helped in the formation of scientific attitudes.

Kulakarni (1975) found that the work experience was effective in inculcating in the pupils love of scientific attitude.

Studies of Curtis, Blair and Goodson, and Vicklund seem to show that direct teaching does modify the attitudes of young people, and the study made of Curtis gave rather clear evidence that pupils who engage in wide reading in general science develop scientific attitudes more than those who study only single subject.

The scientific attitudes which have been explored are attributes of intellectually and emotionally mature individuals, persons who not only behave outwardly in desirable ways but also understand why they act as they do. To develop attitudes, Klausmeier suggests eight steps that the teachers can take to facilitate the learning of attitudes. These may be interpreted in terms of the problems of science teaching in the following manner.

1. The attitude to be taught must be identified.
2. The meanings of the vocabulary used to describe attitudes or the behaviours related to them must be clarified for the learner.
3. Informative experience about the attitude object should be provided. In the case of scientific attitudes these objects are usually the various situations that occur in the problem-solving process. Typical of these are: (a) the sensing of the problem in a perplexing situation, (b) clarifying and defining the problem, (c) formulating of hypotheses (d) reasoning out the consequences of the hypotheses and the designing of investigations, (e) gathering of data, (f) treating and interpreting of data, (g) generalizing or drawing conclusions, and (h) communicating the results of the investigation to others. Students need to be instructed in the performance of each of these steps and in their relationships to the various attitudes that characterize the scientifically minded person. It is so hoped, of course, that pupils will exhibit these attitudes in appropriate situation outside the classroom. To help them generalize these attitudes, teachers can point out the general nature of the attitude object by showing similarities between

scientific problem-solving procedures and the treatment of problematic situations in daily affairs.

4. Desirable identifying figures for the learner should be provided. These models, whether they may be teacher, parents, peers, or historical figures, provide the learner with ready-made behaviours which he can use as his first attempts at the desired behaviour.
5. Pleasant emotional experiences should accompany the learning of the attitudes. Pupils need freedom to attempt their own patterns of exploration and sufficient time to pursue an investigation to the point where they experience the satisfaction that accompanies inquiry and discovery.
6. Appropriate context for practice and confirmation should be arranged. Learning experiences must be selected on the basis of knowledge, skills, and attitudes to be leaned. At times the central theme of a lesson might have to be a particular attitude with other learnings playing secondary roles.
7. Group techniques should be used to facilitate understanding and acceptance. The varied activities possible in well-equipped science rooms permit students to learn as individuals on some occasions and as members of groups of varying sizes on others. Group decision making, that occurs in the planning and carrying out investigations and the evaluation of results, permits a sharing of emotional commitment which can enhance the learning of an attitude.
8. Deliberate cultivation of the desired attitude should also be encouraged. Pupils need to be aware of the behaviours that accompany an attitude and to practice them. Sometimes this requires the difficult task of breaking old habits or of improving poorly learned ones. The teacher must be able to provide guidance for this learning.

There are implications in what has been said for the education of teachers as well as for the instruction of school children. It has often been said that 'you can't teach something you don't know'. A corollary to this generalization might be this; 'pupils cannot learn attitudes that their teachers do not have. It may very well be that the first step in meeting this challenge to science education will consist of an inward look upon our own knowledge and value systems. Science teachers have a responsibility.

It is to them that the public turns for an understanding of science, not just the facts of science, or the skills, but also for a perspective that relates science to all other areas of human experience.

SCIENTIFIC APTITUDE

Scientific aptitude, defined as potentiality for future accomplishment in science without regard to past training and achievement in this field, appears to be dependent upon a variety of factors. These factors are not necessarily unique to potential success in science but may be equally functional in determining success in other areas. Few attempts, therefore, have been made to develop tests of aptitude for the science area alone. The Stanford Scientific Aptitude Test, first published in 1929, does however, represent such an attempt. Ingenious though it is, this test revealed some of the difficulties that beset an individual who undertakes the task of developing an instrument to measure scientific aptitude.

In India, systematic and sustained research is lacking in the field of aptitude testing in general and measurement of scientific aptitude in particular (Sharma, 1980), Nevertheless, after the recommendations of the Secondary Education Commission (1952) were adopted, interest in aptitude testing grew and some independent attempts were made by Indian researchers to standardize scientific aptitude tests and to measure scientific aptitude. The researchers, namely Verma, (1957) Mitra (1963) Choudhari (1965), Nair, *et al.* (1968), Deshponde (1967), Mukherji and Chatterji (1972), Gupta (1975), Ohja (1975), and Sharma (1980) developed their own tests.

Jose (1987) conducted a study by using Kerala University Science Aptitude Test and found that about 70 per cent of 9th class pupils possessed averâge scientific aptitude, and about 15 per cent each possessed high and low scientific aptitude.

The research studies on scientific aptitude indicate that they were studied in correlation with achievement and some other behavioural aspects rather than studying independently. So we can have a look on the relationship between scientific aptitude and achievement in the forthcoming pages of the present review of related research.

3

Research Design

Research design decides the fate of the proposal and its outcome. As such it is regarded as the heart of any research. Designing provides a picture for the whole study before starting of the work. It is, in a simple language, a plan of action. It is therefore desirable to have a methodically designed research plan. In this chapter, the following three aspects have been discussed which are concerned with the design of the present study.

Research Procedures followed

This includes the operational definitions of the different terms used, the various hypotheses that were framed for verification in the present study and the rationale of these hypotheses.

Selection of the sample

This includes the sampling techniques used, the reasons for selection of a particular sampling technique, and the selection of sample according to different variables.

Selection of Tools

This includes the selection of suitable tools for collection of data, description of tools selected, testing their suitability for the present study, and the procedure followed in administering the tools to collect the data required for the present study.

The present study is divided into three areas to study them in depth in a specific and concrete way. The three areas are scientific attitude, scientific aptitude, and the relationship between scientific attitude and scientific aptitude

Taking the objectives into consideration, the following five variables were selected in each of the four sub-areas of the present study.

1. Boys *versus* Girls
2. Private *versus* Government schools
3. Rural *versus* Urban schools
4. English *versus* Telugu media schools
5. Residential *versus* Non-residential schools

The table 3.1 gives a clear picture of the four area of the present study and the variables to be studied under each area.

Table 3.1 : Variables and Areas of the Study

Scientific Attitude	*Scientific Aptitude*	*Association between Scientific Attitude and Scientific Aptitude*
Boys vs. Girls	Boys vs. Girls	Boys vs. Girls
Private vs. Urban Schools	Private vs. Urban Schools	Rural vs. Urban Schools
English vs. Telugu medium Schools	English vs. Telugu medium schools	English vs. Telugu medium schools
Residential vs. Non-Residential Schools	Residential vs. Non-Residential Schools	Residential vs. Non-Residential Schools

After deciding the areas and variables, the tools to be used for collection of data were finalised. To measure the three major aspects of the secondary school pupils, **Scientific Attitude Scale** standardised by J.K. Sood and R.P. Sanadhya to measure scientific attitude, **Kerala University Science Aptitude Test** standardised by Nàir, et al. to measure the scientific aptitude of secondary school pupils were taken into consideration. After verifying the validity and reliability of the translated tools, they were finally selected for the use in the present study.

The population for the present study consisted of the tenth class pupils of Guntur district of Andhra Pradesh. From this population, a representative sample had to be selected. After a detailed study of the different techniques of sampling, the **Stratified Sampling Technique** was found to be the most suitable one and was used for the collection of data. A sample of 600 secondary school tenth class pupils was selected through this stratified sampling technique by taking the different variables under study into consideration. The data were collected from the sample and the school authorities personally.

Hypotheses were formulated for testing in the present study. The hypotheses formulated will be presented in the forth coming pages of this chapter for discussion along with their rationale supporting the study.

Before going into the details of the sample, sampling techniques, tools, it is worthwhile to discuss the operational definitions of the key terms used in the present study which will enlighten the characteristics involved in each term.

OPERATIONAL DEFINITIONS OF THE KEY TERMS

The operational definitions of the important terms used in the present study are discussed and defined herewith.

Scientific Attitude

Since the beginning of the present century science educators have included the development of scientific attitude among the general aims of science education. Some writers label this attitude as "scientific mindedness" (Burnett, 1944), "that habit of scientific thinking" (Noll, 1933) or "the spirit of science" (Educational Policies Commission, 1966) and it is most often characterised by a list of component attitudes such as objectivity, open-mindedness, scepticism, and a willingness to suspend judgement if there is insufficient evidence" (Okay, 1982).

The scientific attitude, by its very name, tends to be associated solely with the area of science. There is a general agreement among investigators that a person who has a scientific point of view (1) looks for the natural causes of events; (2) is open-minded toward the work and opinion of others and toward information related to his problem; (3) bases opinions and conclusions on adequate evidence; (4) evaluates techniques and procedures used and information obtained; and (5) is curious concerning the things he observes.

Richard H. Lampkin, Jr. (1938) through an extensive study brought out 92 scientific attitudes. They are presented in different groups, the groups are:

1. Applicability of the Scientific Method
2. Sensitivity of Perception
3. Accuracy of Perception
4. Objectivity of Perception
5. Limitation of Perception
6. Scientific Classification
7. Sampling
8. Nature of Scientific Law
9. Nature of Hypothesis
10. Formation of Laws and Hypotheses
11. No possible proof
12. Compatibility with Accepted concepts
13. Test by Experiment
14. Guarding against Error
15. Persistent Search for Adequate conceptions
16. Mind open to necessary change

The second study of Lampkin revealed that there had been fairly general recognition and acceptance of the scientific attitudes grouped under the following topics.

1. Applicability of the scientific method.
2. Limitation of perception.
3. Materials of science are drawn from sensitive, accurate and objective perception.
4. Hypotheses and laws must be compatible with accepted concepts.
5. Test by experiment.
6. Guarding against error.
7. Persistent search for adequate conceptions.

Also, it is shown that the attitudes under the following heads, according to Lampkin, had been neglected almost completely. They are:

1. Laws and hypotheses are based on sampling of experience.
2. No conception can be demonstrated to be necessarily true.

Similarly, there were other attitudes which had been recognised after a fashion, but evidently had been understood in senses quite different from those developed in this study. Such attitudes are included in the groups under the following categories:

1. Nature of scientific law
2. Nature of hypothesis
3. Formulation of laws and hypotheses
4. Necessity of renouncing emotion in scientific work

According to Ebel (1938) the accepted elements of scientific attitude were classified in terms of their common characteristics and arranged in accordance with the relations existing between them. In stating each element an effort was made to use clear, concise terminology. Because of the fact that there are not separate names available for each of the elements of the scientific attitude. It was necessary to refer to them in terms of their influence on behaviour. Hence the word "readiness" is used to indicate a mental set which inclines the individual to certain types of behaviour. Thus the statement, "Readiness to be open-minded", might be translated as, "A metal set which inclines the individual to be open-minded". "Open -mindedness" describes the behaviour; "Readiness to be open-minded" describes the attitude.

Noll (1935) opined that the scientific attitude includes the following habits of thinking.

1. Habit of accuracy in all operations, including accuracy in calculation, observation and report.
2. Habit of intellectual honesty.
3. Habit of open-mindedness
4. Habit of suspended judgement.
5. Habit of looking for true cause and effect relationship.
6. Habit of criticalness, including that of self-criticism.

The titles as listed, according to Noll, are probably sufficient to describe the habit in detail.

They may, however, be briefly defined for further clarity in terms of their opposites:

1. Accuracy in calculation, observation, and report in the opposite of habits of careless, inaccurate work.

2. Intellectual honesty in the opposite of bigotry, prejudice and intolerance.
4. Suspended judgement is the opposite of the habit of making snap judgements or of jumping to conclusions.
5. Looking for true cause and effect relationship is the opposite of habits of superstitious thinking of expecting rewards to come without commensurate effort.
6. The habit of criticalness including that of self-criticism is the opposite of habits of accepting explanations of phenomena without question, or without attempt at evaluation; it is the opposite of the habit of condoning and accepting such things as racketeering political corruption, and the like, as inevitable.

Noll also listed fourteen specific objectives without any attempt to rank them. The fourteen specific objectives are-

1. Command of factual information.
2. Familiarity with laws, principles and theories.
3. Ability to distinguish between fact and theory.
4. Concept of cause and effect relationship.
5. Ability to make observations.
6. Habit of basing judgement on fact.
7. Ability to formulate workable hypotheses.
8. Willingness to change opinion on the basis of new evidence.
9. Freedom from superstitions.
10. Appreciation of the contributions of science to our civilization.
11. Appreciation of natural beauty.
12. Appreciation of man's place in the universe.
13. Appreciation of the possible future developments of science.
14. Possession of interest in science.

Davis tried to bring out brief and accurate list of elements of scientific attitude. He prepared a questionnaire with a list of characteristics. He sent them to 250 well-trained experienced teachers. He ranked the characteristics as selected by these experienced teachers, and finally accepted those which were chosen by at least 80 per cent of them. The following are the characteristics which are finally selected.

1. Willingness to change opinion on the basis of evidence (92%).
2. Search for the whole truth regardless of personal, religious or social prejudice (89%).
3. Concept of cause and effect relationship (86%).
4. Habit of basing judgement on fact (85%).
5. Power or ability to distinguish between fact and theory (82%).
6. Freedom from superstitious beliefs (81%).

According to National Society for the Study of Education, Scientific attitudes can be defined a open-mindedness a desire for accurate knowledge, confidence in procedures for seeking knowledge, and the expectation that the solution of the problem will come through the use of verified knowledge.

Heiss, Obourn and Hoffman stated the following qualities of a person with scientific attitude-

1. Looks for the natural causes for things that happen:
   a) does not believe in superstitions, such as charms of good or bad luck.
   b) Believes that there is no connection necessarily between two events just because they happen at the same time or one after the other.
2. Is open-minded towards works and opinions of others and information related to his problem:
   a) believes that truth never changes, but his ideas of what is true may change as he gains better understanding of that truth.
   b) revises his opinions and conclusions in the light of additional reliable evidence.
   c) listens to, observes, or reads evidence supporting ideas contrary to his personal opinions.
   d) accepts no conclusion as final or ultimate.
3. Bases opinions and conclusions on adequate evidence:
   a) is slow to accept as fact any thing not supported by convincing proof.

b) bases his conclusions upon evidence obtained from a variety of dependable sources.

c) searches for the most satisfactory explanation of observed phenomenon that the evidence permits.

d) sticks to the facts and avoids exaggeration.

e) does not allow his personal pride, bias, prejudice or ambition to prevent the truth.

f) does not jump to conclusions.

4. Evaluates technique and procedures used and information obtained:

a) uses a planned procedure in solving his problems.

b) seeks to use the various techniques and procedures which have proved valuable in obtaining evidence.

c) seeks to adopt the various techniques and procedures to the problem at hand.

d) personally considers the evidence and besides whether it relates to the problem.

e) judges whether the evidence is sound, sensible and complete enough to allow a conclusion to be drawn.

f) select the most recent, authoritative and accurate evidence related to the problem.

5. Is curious concerning the things he observes:

a) wants to know the 'whys', 'whats', hows' of observed phenomenon.

b) is not satisfied with vague explanations of these questions.

Bhaskara Rao, et al. (1989) state the most useful scientific attitudes are open mindedness, critical mindedness, respect for evidence, suspended judgement, intellectual honesty, willingness to change opinion, search for truth, curiosity, rational thinking, etc.

Caldwell and Curtis (1943) gave the following list of scientific attitudes-

1. A curiosity to know about one's environment.
2. The belief that nothing can happen without a cause and those occurrences that seem strange and mysterious can always be explained by natural causes.

3. An unwillingness to accept as facts any statements that are not supported by convincing proof.
4. The determination not to believe in superstitions of any sort.
5. The belief that truth itself never changes, but that our ideas of what is true change as we gain more and more knowledge.
6. An intention not to experiment on to work blindly and carelessly, but to begin only after careful observation.
7. The determination to be careful and accurate in all one's observations.
8. A willingness to consider all the evidence and try to decide whether it really relates to the matter which is being considered, whether it is sound and sensible, and whether it is complete enough to allow a conclusion to be made.
9. A determination not to base final conclusions on one or a few observations, but to work as long as may be necessary in order to secure answer to a problem.
10. The desire to do one's own observation and experimentation but a willingness to use results of other scientists' work.
11. The willingness to change an opinion or a conclusion if later evidence shows that it is wrong.
12. The intention to respect another's point of view.
13. The determination to prevent one's own likes and dislikes from influencing one's judgement.

Vaidya (1976) includes (1) Open-mindedness, (2) Curiosity, (3) Judgement, (4) Willingness to test and verify conclusions, (5) Faith in cause and effect relationship, (6) Honest reporting, (7) Rejection of the principle of authority, and lastly (8) More faith in the books written by specialists in their respective fields on scientific attitude.

Sharma includes the characteristics in scientific attitude like (1) Criticalness in observation, (2) Open-mindedness, (3) respectfulness for other's views, (4) Curiosity to know, (5) Objectivity in approach, (6) Opposition to superstitions, (7) suspending judgement until the availability of suitable evidence, (8) Impartiality in judgements, etc.

For purpose of identification, Diederich described some of the components of scientific attitude such as - (1) Scepticism. Not taking things for granted, (2) Faith in the possibility of solving problems, (3)

Desire for experimental verification, (4) Precision, (5) A liking for new things, (6) Willingness to change opinions, (7) Humanity (8) Loyalty to truth, (9) An objective attitude (10) Aversion to superstition, (11) Liking for specific explanations, (12) Desire for completeness of knowledge, (13) Suspended judgement, (14) distinguishing between hypotheses and solutions, (15) Awareness of assumptions, (16) Judgement of what is of fundamental and general significance, (17) Respect for theoretical structures, (18) Respect for quantification, (19) Acceptance of probabilities, and (20) Acceptance of warranted generalisations.

Like the above, lists and definitions about scientific attitude are not exhaustive. Hundreds of articles, research studies in various areas came into existence discussing the scientific attitude, its role in education, and its development. After going through all of these lists and definitions, the attitudes such as rationality, curiosity, open-mindedness, aversion to superstitions, objectivity of intellectual beliefs and suspended judgement were taken into consideration to select the scientific attitude scale for the present study.

SCIENTIFIC APTITUDE

The term aptitude is differently defined by different psychologists, as many case do happen, but these different definitions agree in certain essentials such as 'present ability', 'role of training', 'case of acquiring proficiency', 'interest in activity', and so on.

In the Dictionary of Education (1959) aptitude is denied as a pronounced innate capacity for or ability in a given line of endeavour such as a particular art, school subject or vocation'. Thus in this definition an aptitude refers to an individual's inborn capacities or potentialities which are indicative of some special abilities. According to English and English (1958) it may be regarded as the capacity to acquire proficiency with a given amount of training.' Aptitude in Great Illustrated Dictionary (1984) is defined as "a natural talent, skill or ability, quickness in learning and understanding". Here in the above two definitions it has been emphasised that an aptitude refers to the capacity of an individual to be skilled in some work receiving formal or informal training.

Freeman (1965) has defined an aptitude as a combination of characteristics indicative of an individual's capacity to acquire (with training) some specific knowledge, skill or set or organised responses such as the ability to speak a language, to become a musician, to do mechanical work'. Freeman has also pointed out that the aptitude is different trom skill and proficiency. Freeman has further stated that... 'when we speak of an individual's aptitude for a given type of activity we mean the capacity to acquire proficiency under as revealed by his performance on selected tests that have predictive value.' In other words the most important factor is an aptitude, i.e., the capacity to acquire proficiency. On the other hand if an individual has no aptitude for a particular type of task, he will not be skilled or proficient in that task in spite of training given to him. These aptitudes refer to an individual's inborn capacity to acquire proficiency in a given area of human endeavour. The aptitude is a capacity in any given skill or field of knowledge, on the basis of which a prediction may be made regarding the amount of improvement which further training might effect.

Majority of the psychologists agree on the point that the aptitudes are innate. Nevertheless it is also realised that attitudes are influenced by the environment in which the individual lives. In other words, though aptitudes are innate and mostly governed by hereditary factors, yet environmental factors also play an important role. As a matter of fact, the biological and cultural factors are involved in all psychological activities of an individual.

The aptitudes are fairly constant for a period of time. Variations occur within the framework of environmental factors as it is generally believed that aptitudes like 'intelligent Quotient are constant. But according to Wrightstone, et al. (1956) 'while the evidence is conflicting, the trend seems to be in the direction of assuming that aptitudes are some what variable and are affected within limits by educational and environmental influences'.

Educators had first considered aptitude as unitary, i.e., a function of a single general trait or characteristic. But factor analystic technique indicates that an aptitude need not necessarily be the function of a single general trait. T. L. Kelly (1928) identified verbal, number memory, spatial, reasoning, deduction and induction abilities which were indicative of pluralistic aptitudes.

Before the second world war there were small scale attempts to find out the important dimensions of scientific aptitude and the development of techniques for the prediction of success in science. But later, an increased effort was made to develop techniques to identify and locate students with science aptitude for professional and specialised courses, programmes, etc.

Scientific aptitude is complex of interacting hereditary and environmental determinants producing predispositions or abilities. We can identify to an extent, certain, not all, characteristics possessed by individuals who succeed late in scientific endeavour. Dressel (1963) defines 'scientific aptitude as potentiality for future accomplishment in science without regard to past training and achievement.

Super states that 'scientific aptitude is presumably largely an intellectual matter, and it seems that battery of tests for the selection of promising scientists will stress such factors as reasoning, spatial visualization, number ability, scientific vocabulary and mechanical comprehension are too less pure aptitudes which should also be significant'.

Scientific aptitude appears to be dependent upon a variety of factors. The presence of certain study skills; persistence in learning, motivation; satisfactions derived from learning a subject, socio-economic factors and cultural back ground are some of the important determinants of scientific aptitude. Factors like physical development, interests, attitudes are also be considered necessary for science aptitude.

Much of the literature concerning scientific aptitude has centered upon two major questions - (1) can scientific aptitude be represented in terms of a single defined entity?, (2) What are its distinguishing components if scientific aptitude is an unitary variable. Brandwein (1955) viewed scientific aptitude not as a single trait but as one of the aspects of general intelligence. In the opinion of Miles (1954), scientific aptitude is another example of a talent present in the gifted group so far greater extent than its probable realization in adult achievement. The important components, according to Guilford (1950), of scientific aptitude are sensitivity to problems, ability to develop novel ideas and the ability evaluate.

Scientific Aptitude Test

There are a number of aptitude tests in as may branches as the education and employment have. Generally the aptitude test makers follow two methods. In the first method, a particular profession or occupation is studied and analysed with a view to making an aptitude test. Thus, the analysis of an occupation enables the test maker to have a list of items which refers to the various aspects of abilities needed for an occupation. On the basis of this list the aptitude test for that occupation is prepared. Commenting on this type of aptitude test Jane Warters (1954) states that such tests are small scale tasks that involve abilities which are the same as or similar to the ones required for the performance of a particular work or activity for which aptitude is being measured. This type of test if often useful for selecting workers. It is not very useful in a students personal work because effective use costs too much in both time and equipment.

The second method employed by aptitude test makers takes into account the important factors necessary for success in an occupation. Thus efforts are made to measure the important components of an occupation. In other words, independent tests are prepared for each important factor involved in a particular occupations or fields. Individually the tests may not be very valid for predicting success in a particular activity or field, but all are a number combined to give a good basis for prediction. It may be noted here that the second method has been widely used in the preparation of aptitude tests.

According to Encyclopedic Dictionary and Directory of Education (1987) aptitude test is a test designed to measure the potential ability of a person for performing a certain type of capacity.

It is a capacity test as a mathematics aptitude test or a musical aptitude test. An aptitude test is a standardised test designed to measure the ability of an individual to develop skills or acquire knowledge. Aptitude Tests (Best) attempt to predict the degree of achievement that may be expected from individuals in a particular activity to the extent that they measure past learning.

Scientific aptitude test is a test meant for the assessment of the ability of an individual's performance in science. Here, in the present study, it is meant for the measurement of secondary school pupils' aptitude in science.

Scientific Attitude Scale

Social psychologists focused on attitudes as a central concept in seeking to develop their field a scientific discipline. Indeed attitudes seem so pervasive that their study might be said to cover the full range of human behaviour and experience. People tend to develop attitudes toward whatever they experience toward other people, toward political and religious institutions, toward moral and philosophical systems, toward science and arts, apparently toward everything. Yet often enough, attitudes fail to stand the test of logical scrutiny as each person seems to be a bundle of prejudice.

The attitude are predispositions to classify sets of objects or events and to react to them with some degree of evaluative consistency. While attitudes logically are hypothetical constructs (i.e., they are inferred but not objectively observable), they are manifested in conscious experience, verbal reports, gross behaviour and physiological symptoms.

An Attitude test (Best) is a test designed to measure the motional pattern of likes and dislikes of a person, mostly in relation to personal adjustments.

The information-form that attempts to the measurement of scientific attitudes of an individual is a scientific attitude scale. In the present study, the scientific attitude scale was employed to study the scientific attitudes of secondary school pupils.

Private Schools

The schools managed by private organisations or persons, either partially or totally, were included in private schools. The public schools, Government recognised and aided schools were also included under private schools.

Government Schools

The schools under the sole management of Government were included under Government schools. So the schools managed by Zilla Praja Parishads, Municipalities or Government were included in this category.

Urban Schools

The schools located in an urban area were considered urban schools. An urban area should satisfy the following conditions. (1) It should have a municipal corporation, cantonment board or notified town area committee, etc. (2) It should have a minimum population of five thousand. (3) Atleast 75% of its male working population should be engaged in non agricultural pursuits. (4) It should have a population of at least 400 persons per square kilometer.

Rural Schools

The schools located in rural area were considered as rural schools. A rural area should have a population below five thousand, with 75% of the population engaged in agricultural pursuits.

Residential Schools

The pupils should stay on the school premises with their teachers instead of coming from their houses daily. So they spend all their time either on the school campus or in the hostels and pursue studies under the constant supervision of teachers. Such schools were considered residential schools.

Non-residential Schools

The pupils of these schools will only be in the school campus during instructional hours and spend their remaining time at home or at other place. Such schools were considered non-residential schools.

VARIABLES OF THE STUDY

The variables considered for the present study are: (1) Boys versus girls, (2) Private versus government Schools, (3) Rural versus urban Schools, (4) English versus Telugu medium schools, and (5) Residential versus Non-residential Schools. The rationale for choosing the above stated variables is discussed herewith.

Boys *versus* Girls

Sex was taken as a variable to see if there is any significant difference between boys and girls in possessing scientific attitude and scientific aptitude.

In olden days, the boys were educated and the girls were restricted to their kitchens by their adult community. Times changed and the adults recognised the importance of women education. In the words of our late Prime Minister Pandit Jawaharlal Nehru, "If you educate a man you educate only one person; if you educate a women you educate the entire family". In the course of time women's education gained importance and many parents are encouraging their daughters to pursue higher education, and even allowing them to go aboard. The women are also showing excellence in all fields. Their presence is felt almost in all fields.

As the physiological conditions, exposure to society, education and other aspects of girls and boys vary differently, there may be a significant difference in the possession of scientific attitude and scientific aptitude. The boys may be exposed to the society to a larger extent, but the girls spend most of their time in going through books or helping their parents at home. These factors will show their influence on their mental development.

It is especially important to study the level of possession of scientific attitude and scientific aptitude of secondary school pupils because they just enter the adolescent stage, which is otherwise knows as the period of stress and strain. At this stage, this sample finds it extremely difficult to adjust themselves in the society because they are accepted neither as adults nor as children. It is also familiar that girls mature faster than boys at the early adolescent stage, both physically and mentally. The above factors will have their own impact on the possession of scientific attitude and scientific aptitude.

So, a comparison between boys and girls will reveal of any difference exists in the possession of scientific attitude and scientific aptitude.

English Medium Schools *versus* Telugu Medium Schools

Usually people feel that there may not be much more difference between the students of Telugu medium and English medium. But many studies in various fields proved that the pupils studying the their mother tongue score better because they understand anything without any hindrance. For those pupils who are studying in English medium here will be a communication gap or delay in understanding a phenomenon owing to language hindrance. So there will be a difference between Telugu medium pupils and English medium pupils. Hence, this variable is taken into consideration to see what will be the difference between these two groups in the level of possession of scientific attitude and scientific aptitude.

Private Schools *versus* Government Schools

The reputation of private schools is generally better when compared with that of the government schools. In private schools the pupils are exposed to better conditions and better study atmosphere. The school laboratory and library facilities, etc., will be better. If better facilities are not provided in private schools, the parents will question the authorities concerned, because they pay higher fees for their children. The laboratory and library facilities will play a major role in the possession of scientific attitude and scientific aptitude.

The quality of teaching is also supposed to be better in private schools. The teachers take more interest in teaching in private schools as they are always either in the fear of losing their jobs or immediately being questioned by the managements about the quality of their teaching. Since the standard of possession of scientific attitude and scietific aptitude will be different.

Thus, it is important to study about the difference in the possession of scientific attitude and scientific aptitude in private and goverriment schools.

Rural Schools *versus* Urban Schools

The urban schools are well equipped in many aspects when compared with the rural schools. The buildings, the libraries, the laboratories, the teaching staff, the educational atmosphere, the competitive spirit among the pupils, the amenities provided to pupils to pursue education, the exposure to science fairs, exhibitions, workshops, the student participation in teaching learning process, the use of audio-visual aids, etc., will always be better in urban schools than in rural schools. The library and laboratory facilities, use of audio-visual aids in teaching, and the better teachers will play a commandable role in the acquisition of scientific attitude and scientific aptitude.

A comparison between rural and urban school pupils will bring out the difference in the level of possession of scientific attitude and scientific aptitude, if there is any.

Residential Schools *versus* Non-Residential Schools

The residential schools are supposed to be in better position in all aspects when compared with non-residential school. The pupils of the residential schools stay in the school itself without going home after the regular classroom teaching learning activities. They stay with their teachers all the time, except for a few hours, and study and clear off their doubts immediately either in the classroom or during the study hours. Contrary to this, the pupils of the non-residential school stay outside the school, except for 5 or 6 hours, and spend their time at their own sweet will and interest. The pupils interested in studies usually get some doubts during their study at home, but they have to wait for quite long time to clear them off. The delay in getting them cleared off sometimes leads to carelessness or frustration. This teaching learning aspect will definitely play an important role in the possession of scientific attitude and scientific aptitude.

The infra-structural and the library and laboratory facilities will also be better in residential schools. In Andhra Pradesh, Residential Schools were started offering best education to the pupils by providing facilities conducive to the progress of each and every student. The intelligent pupils will always be in a better position, because they are not mixed up with lesser intelligent pupils, which is a practice in non-residential schools.

Considering the above facts, the pupils of residential and non-residential type of school are taken into consideration to study the level of possession of scientific attitude and scientific aptitude.

HYPOTHESES OF THE STUDY

The major areas covered by the major hypotheses are scientific aptitude, and independence of scientific attitude and scientific aptitude. Each one of the main hypotheses has been studied in further detail by forming five sub-hypotheses under each head.

HYPOTHESIS 1

Secondary School Pupils Will Possess High Scientific Attitude

The scientific attitude, by its very name, tends to be associated solely with the area or science and scientific methods. Actually, the scientific attitude is applicable to nearly every situation an individual may encounter in the subjects in the curriculum.

An individual who has learned the scientific attitude and makes use of its does not jump to conclusions. He is patient and reserved in his judgement. In considering a situation or problem he studies all aspects of it, looking at every side of it before approaching the study with a minimum of prejudice or bias. Although he may have previous knowledge, he will not have preconceived notions unless they have basis in this objective understanding of the problem. The person possessing scientific attitude has no time for old wives' tales, rumours or superstitions. He is a person of caution who observes carefully before coming to a conclusion. He is ready and willing to change his mind when he observes new evidence that he can accept as valid. The scientific attitude is also reflected in the individual who bases his actions, thoughts and conduct on the knowledge that is available to him, and who suspends reaching and conduct on the knowledge that is available to him, and who suspends reaching conclusions and forming judgements when reliable and objective information is lacking, or until such time as he has the opportunity to study such information.

One of the goals of the school programme is the development of the scientific attitude. Its development in pupils leads to a willingness to the use of many sources for locating valid information. Critical thinking in evaluating and applying such information is also closely allied to the scientific attitude. "Pupils experienced in the use of the scientific attitude are willing to experiment, patient in checking the results of their experiments, and questioning as they conduct their experiments. Individuals without a proper attitude toward the application of knowledge or the acquisition of new knowledge gain little value for their education. Those with the scientific attitude have a means of applying their knowledge and a thirst for new knowledge"

Each day learning and living in the school affords multitudes of opportunities for developing the scientific attitude in school community. The scientific attitude is not one that simply comes with maturity, it must be encouraged, practised and emphasised during the learning process. Careful planning is one of the most helpful ways of guiding students in the development of such an attitude. A course of study or a syllabus need not be confirming, but such guides can offer many needed ideas, concepts and facts that will aid the teacher and the pupil with their planning. If a course of study or other guide is lacking, co-operative planning can led to areas that the class, guided by the teacher, wishes to pursue.

There is an evidence of growing scientific attitude. The seventh grader will undoubtedly show more evidence of the scientific attitude than the fifth or second grader, but if all teachers pointedly work toward the development of such an attitude, it will be evident throughout the child's school years. The first-grader who checks his teacher's statements at home may be less impatient than curious. The tenth grader who takes time to prove his science problems is certainly showing that he wishes to check his results carefully. The desire to seek more information in a class discussion, certainly, have consulted references for information. The young pupil who laughs at superstitions, because he realizes that nothing happens without some cause, has mastered more of the scientific attitudes than many adults.

Although many of the characteristics that we associate with the scientific attitude may develop naturally with maturity. The open-mind, cautious, objective approach to situations that require decisions based on reliable evidence should be encouraged and emphasized by each teacher with proper attention to its development. The scientific attitude can be fostered as a characteristic valuable to each student as he faces problems in schools and in adult life.

As stated earlier, under the area of scientific attitude the variables-sex, private versus government schools, rural versus urban schools, Telugu medium versus English medium schools and residential versus non-residential school were considered. To study each of these variables in detail the following sub-hypotheses were formulated. They were stated in "null hypothesis" form. 'A null hypothesis states that there is no significant difference or relationship between two or more parameters. It concerns are true differences or whether they merely result from sampling error.

Hypothesis 1 A

There is no significant difference between the level of scientific attitude possessed by boys and girls of secondary schools.

Hypothesis 1 B

There is no significant difference between the level of scientific attitude possessed by the pupils of private and government secondary schools.

Hypothesis 1 C

There is no significant difference in the level of scientific attitude possessed by the pupils of private and government secondary schools.

Hypothesis 1 D

There is no significant difference in the level of scientific attitude possessed by the English medium and Telugu medium pupils of secondary schools.

Hypothesis 1 E

There is no significant difference in the level of scientific attitude possessed by the pupils of residential and non-residential secondary schools.

HYPOTHESIS 2

Secondary School Pupils will Possess High Scientific Aptitude

Before 1930s there were small scale attempts made to find out the important dimensions of scientific aptitude and the development of techniques for the prediction of success in science. Later, an increased effort was made to develop techniques to identify and locate students with scientific aptitude.

Scientific aptitude is a complex of interacting hereditary and environmental determinants producing predispositions or abilities in science. One can identify only some, but not all, the characteristics possessed by individuals who will succeed in scientific endeavour in their later lives. Dressel defines scientific aptitude as potentiality for future accomplishment in science without regard to past training and achievement. Scientific aptitude, then, appears to be dependent upon a variety of factors. It consists of more mental capacity. The presence of certain study skills; persistence factors in learning and motivation; satisfaction derived from learning the subject; socio-economic factors and cultural background are some of the important determinants of scientific aptitude. Factors like physical development, moral character, interests and attitudes may also be considered necessary for scientific aptitude.

Under scientific aptitude, the following five sub-hypotheses were framed.

Hypothesis 2 A

There is no significant difference between the level of scientific aptitude possessed by boys and girls of secondary schools.

Hypothesis 2 B

There is no significant difference between the level of scientific aptitude possessed by the pupils of private and governmental secondary schools.

Hypothesis 2 C

There is no significant difference in the level of scientific aptitude possessed by the pupils of rural and urban secondary schools.

Hypothesis 2 D

There is no significant difference in the level of scientific aptitude possessed by the English medium and Telugu medium pupils secondary schools.

Hypothesis 2 E

There is no significant difference in the level of scientific aptitude possessed by the pupils of residential and non-residential secondary schools.

HYPOTHESIS 3

There will be a significant positive association between scientific attitude and scientific aptitude of secondary school pupils

Under the area of association between scientific attitude and scientific aptitude of secondary school pupils, the following five sub-hypotheses were framed.

Hypothesis 3 A

There is no significant association between scientific attitude and scientific aptitude of boys and girls of secondary school pupils.

Hypothesis 3 B

There is no significant association between scientific attitude and scientific aptitude of pupils of private and government secondary schools.

Hypothesis 3 C

There is no significant association between scientific attitude and scientific aptitude of the pupils of rural and urban secondary schools.

Hypothesis 3 D

There is no significant association between scientific attitude and scientific aptitude of English medium and Telugu medium pupils of secondary schools.

Hypothesis 3 E

There is no significant association between scientific attitude and scientific aptitude of the pupils of residential and non-residential secondary schools.

SELECTION OF SAMPLE

After finalizing the variables of the present study, consideration was given to whether the entire population is to be made the subject for data collection or a particular group is to be selected as representative of the whole population. The 'entire population' here refers to all the tenth class students of the secondary schools of Guntur district of Andhra Pradesh

Of the two techniques, the second one namely, the selection of a group as a representative of the whole population was found to be more convenient and suitable. This technique leads to a considerable saving of time, effort and finance. The number of pupils selected is small, and so it is possible to make a detailed and intensive study. This generally leads to more accurate and reliable results. As this sampling technique has many advantages, it was selected for the collection of data.

In any social research, various methods are utilised for selection and drawing of samples. After a detailed study of all these methods and considering the variables selected for the research work, the stratified sampling method was found to be most suitable.

In the stratified sampling method, the entire population is divided into smaller homogeneous groups (Best) or strata, and then the sample is selected within each group. Every sampling unit in the population is placed in one of the strata prior to the selection of the sample so that the sum of the strata is identical with the population.

Stratified sampling method has certain merits and advantages as a technique of sampling. Auckoff has rightly said that 'stratified sampling enables the researcher to make a comparison of properties of the strata as well as to estimate population characteristics' (Kerlinger, 1964).

In this stratified sampling method, the investigator has greater control over the selection of the sample when compared with random sampling. In random sampling, although every group has a chance of being selected and included in the sample, there is every possibility, and sometimes it does happen, that certain important groups are left unrepresented. But in stratified sampling method no important group is likely to be left out.

Stratified sampling method is the ideal one when comparison between different variables has to be made. For example, if comparison has to be made between private and government school pupils or rural and urban pupils, it would be very difficult to select the required number of units through any other method of sampling. If any other method is used, the problem of bias and prejudice creeps in.

Replacement of units is also possible in the stratified sampling method. Normally if a particular unit is not accessible for a study, it is difficult to replace it by another, but in this method it is possible. Stephen states that 'stratification automatically brings about a replacement of persons lost to the sample, by persons of the same stratum, thus partly correcting the bias that would result if there were no replacement of loses'. As the entire population is divided into particular strata it is easy and convenient to replace an inaccessible case by an accessible one.

In this stratified sampling method, much depends on the stratification process. The following precautions were taken while stratifying the population : the variables involved in the study were taken note of; care was taken to see that each stratum in the universe was large enough in size so that selection of items could be done on random basis; the strata formed were definite and clear cut; each stratum was free from influence of the other; that there was no overlapping.

Before actually selecting the sample, certain fundamental principles were considered to make the sample scientific and clear-cut.

Firstly, the 'universe' was clearly defined. In the technical phraseology of research, the whole population out of which the samples are selected is known as the 'universe'. For the present research work, the universe includes all the students to tenth class studying in secondary schools of Guntur District of Andhra Pradesh. The study was limited to a particular geographical area to facilitate appropriate sample selection and to avoid bias and prejudice.

According to the second principle, decision has to be made about the units of the sample. A unit of sample may be a house, a family, a group of individuals or a single individual. A good unit should possess the following characteristics—*(A) Clarity :* The unit should be clearly defined in unambiguous terms. This would make the study easy and efficient. For the present research work, a sampling unit was defined as a pupil of tenth class studying in any school of Guntur district; *(B) Suitability :* A good unit should be well suited to the problem under study. Since the problem is the possession and comparison of scientific attitude, scientific aptitude and achievement in biology of tenth class pupils of Guntur district, the unit selected is well suited to the problem; *(C) Accessibility :* The unit selected should be easily accessible to the researcher. If the units selected are difficult to reach and if we fail to make use of them, the study would be vitiated. The selected sampling unit i.e., a tenth class pupil is easily accessible since he/she could be approached in any secondary school.

The third principle to be considered while selecting a sample is the availability and preparation of the source list. This is an important factor that makes representative selection possible. A source list is the list which contains the names of the units of the universe from which the sample may be selected. It may exist even before the beginning of the project or it may be prepared afresh by the investigator himself. Without a source list, study through the sampling method is not possible. For the present research work, a source list consisting of the names of schools in the Guntur District was used. Care was taken to see that the source list was up-to-date and valid and that there was no repetition of names of the schools. This source was found to be relevant and suitable because it included high schools as the study deals with the tenth class pupils.

Besides considering these principles, it is extremely important to think about the size of the sample to be selected. If the sample is either too small or too large, it will make the study difficult and also make the results untenable. According to Parten, an optimum sample in survey is one which fulfils the requirements of effective representativeness, reliability and flexibility. The sample should be small enough to avoid intolerable sampling error'. The size of sample for the present research work was decided after considering the following factors.

Since an intensive study was planned, a very large number of samples were not selected. In case of an intensive study, very large number of samples are not so useful as they involve huge consumption of the resources. A smaller sample is convenient.

The size and selection of the samples will also be influenced by the nature of the universe. If the universe is homogeneous, even a small-sized sample may yield dependable and required results. If the universe is heterogeneous, small-sized samples may not be useful. In case of the present study, the heterogeneous universe was split into smaller homogeneous groups and the samples were selected from these strata. For example, all the tenth class pupils of Guntur District were broadly grouped under rural and urban pupils. A sample was selected from each of these two groups.

The investigator needs to determine the number of the groups to be formed. In case the number of groups proposed is large, the size of the samples shall have to be large so that every group should be of proper size and suit the requirements of the study. In case the number of groups proposed is small, even small-sized samples can fulfil the requirement. In the case of the present study, the number of groups into which the universe was divided are—girls and boys, private and government schools, rural and urban schools, English medium and Telugu medium schools, and residential and non-residential schools. Since the number of groups are more, a reasonably large sample was selected from each of these groups.

Practical considerations and accuracy also play a vital role in determining the size of the sample. Every study is guided by certain practical considerations such as time, resources, accessibility of data, etc. Generally, it is believed that a large-sized sample is more representative and generally produces accurate results. This, of course, depends upon the technique of sampling used. If the technique is scientific, even small-sized samples can produce dependable and accurate results. While selecting the size of the sample for the present study, practical considerations like the availability of resources and time were taken into consideration. Care was taken to make the sample selection technique as scientific as possible.

The size of the sample is also governed by the size of the tools to be used. In case the tools are short and the questions asked pertain to certain limited factors, a large sample can be selected. In case the tools are large and the questions complicated, the sample should be small in size so that, from administrative point of view, the investigator may not be put to unnecessary troubles. In the present study, the tools were quite elaborate and large, hence a very large sample was not selected.

The sampling method also determines the size of the sample. When random sampling method is used, the samples have to be large. On the other hand, if samples are selected through stratified sampling method, the reliability can be achieved even with the help of the small-sized samples.

After taking into consideration all these factors which influence the size of the sample, it was decided that an ideal sample would consist of six hundred pupils. This sample is small enough to avoid unnecessary expenditure and large enough to avoid intolerable sampling errors.

After deciding about the sampling method and the size of the sample, the universe selected was divided into different strata. The variables chosen for the study were considered to divide the universe.

Taking the variable which compares rural and urban areas at first instance, the Universe which geographically consisted of Guntur District was split into rural and urban areas. An equal number of sample was taken from both rural and urban areas, i.e., 300 from rural and 300 from urban secondary schools.

The sample from the rural areas had to be selected from the tenth class pupils of Zilla Praja Parishad high schools, Private High Schools and Andhra Pradesh Residential Schools. The two A.P. Residential Schools, one meant for boys and another for girls, were taken into consideration to get the sample for the comparative study of residential and non-residential systems; sixty tenth class pupils were taken from each of these residential schools. To select the sample from the private high schools and Zilla Praja Parishad high schools of rural areas, the random sampling method was considered. In this method all the units from both types of schools were given equal importance. 'The individual observations or individuals are chosen in such a way that each has an equal chance of being selected, and that each choice is independent of any other choice'. Random sampling is done with the help of many methods. The lottery method as suggested by Best is used. In this method the names of all private high schools were written on slips of equal size, the slips were folded round, mixed well and kept in a container. It was decided to select 3 schools from private schools. So three paper slips were picked up from the container and the schools were thus chosen for sampling. Thirty tenth class pupils were taken as sample from each of the three private high schools giving equal importance to both boys and girls. The very sample lottery method was followed to the 3 Zilla Praja Parishad high schools. Thirty tenth class pupils from each school were taken as sample giving equal importance to both boys and girls.

Thus, a total sample of 300 were chosen from rural schools. Out of these, 150 were boys and 150 were girls; 90 were from private high schools and 210 were from government high schools; 120 were from residential schools and 180 were from non-residential schools; and all the sample were of Telugu medium.

Table 3.2 given herewith shows the rural area schools and the number of boys and girls selected from each of them.

Table 3.2 : Sample Distribution in Rural Schools

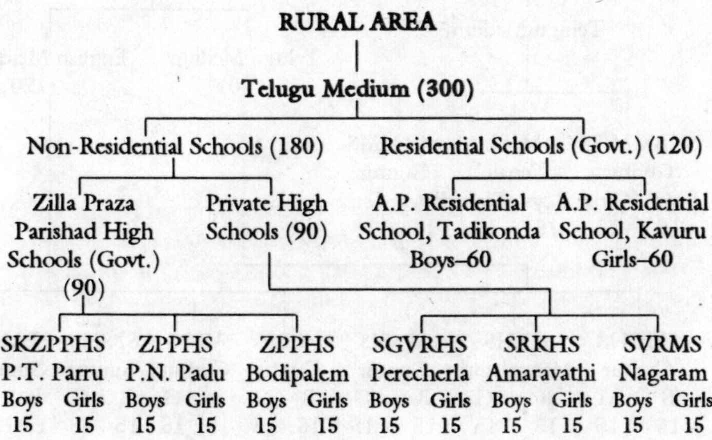

Guntur, Tenali and Mangalagiri towns were chosen as the urban areas for the selection of samples. A source list of all high schools present in these three towns was prepared. Care was taken to see that the list was as exhaustive as possible and included up-to-date information.

After the preparation of the source list of high schools, as all the schools were non-residential, the schools were divided into government and private schools. Further these schools were divided into Telugu medium and English medium schools. Thus 4 categories of schools were formed under the urban area schools. From the four categories of schools, the number of schools selected from each of these categories is—(1) Non-residential, government, Telugu medium schools–3, (2) Non-residential, government, English medium schools–Nil, (3) Non-residential, private, Telugu medium schools–3, and (4) Non-residential, private, English medium schools–4.

Table 3.3 given herewith shows the different categories of urban schools and the number of sample selected from each school.

The government schools selected were less when compared to private schools in urban area, but equal number of Government Telugu

Table 3.3 : Sample Distribution in Urban Schools

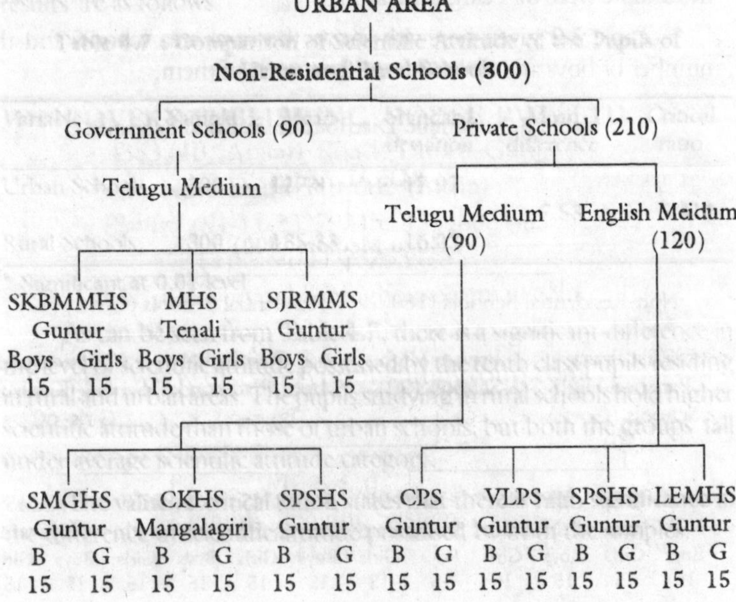

medium and Private Telugu medium schools of urban area were taken for the present study. As there were no English medium schools in rural areas, four English medium schools were selected only from the urban areas to collect the sample. In order to make the sample equal in rural and urban schools, i.e., rural sample 300 and urban sample 300; and to make the equal sample of boys and girls from urban area, i.e., boys sample 150 and girls sample 150; and for equal sample of boys and girls out of total sample i.e., boys sample 300 and girls sample 300, the urban schools were selected accordingly. The total sample of 120 pupils of English medium were selected from the private schools as there were no English medium schools under the management of government in the district. For selecting the different categories of schools of urban areas, the lottery method and random sampling technique, as explained in the case of rural sampling were applied.

The number of pupils selected from each category of school was 30 with equal number of boys and girls, except in the case of Andhra Pradesh Residential schools where 60 pupils were selected from each (boys or girls) school. It was done so because there were only two residential schools in the Guntur district.

The total sample includes—Rural Schools–300; Government Schools–300 and Private Schools–300; Girls–300 and Boys–300; Residential Schools–120 and Non-Residential Schools–480; and English Medium–120 and Telugu Medium–480. The total sample was 600 tenth class pupils studying in Secondary Schools.

The sampling design employed involved not only the stratification of the universe but also random sampling technique to select samples from within the stratum or category.

SELECTION OF TOOLS

A research tool plays a major role in any worthwhile research, as it is the sole factor in determining the sound data and in arriving at perfect conclusions about the problem or study in hand, which, ultimately, helps in providing suitable remedial measures to the problem concerned.

The selection and use of tools can be done in two ways. The first one is to construct a tool independently by the investigator for his own study. Here, there are many problems in doing so. Preparation and standardization of a perfect tool itself is a major task, and one can safely say that it is a doctoral study itself. On construction of their own tools, Anand and Padma (1987) fell that 'A note of caution has to be struck when a researcher develops a tool for his study by merely pooling some items and does not subject it to the sophisticated techniques of tool construction. The result would be then obvious, a poor quality research. With this, one can say that preparation and standardization of tools is a major task, and one should take care in aspects like selection of area and sample, pooling up of statements related to the area and sample, consulting the experts, and application of sophisticated statistical techniques'.

The second way of selection and use of tools is right selection of tools from already standardized ones available in the field of study. Here also it involves a tedious job in locating the tools and identifying their usefulness to the study on hand. Even then, this technique is very useful when a research work is taken to study in depth and when the research work involves a good number of variables. Some people believe that some of the instruments available do not measure up to their standards. Hence new ones. In some instances, consideration should be given to the logistics of the situation. Lacking the time and financial resources of a test and measurement organisation, many researchers cannot expect to produce a better instrument. In these cases, the most logical procedure that he can follow is to choose the best instrument available for his purpose.

Considering the flaws and merits of the selection of tools in either way, the investigator interested in using the standardized tools as the present study involves a thorough study of scientific attitude, scientific aptitude and achievement in biology of secondary school pupils and their association with each other.

Scientific Attitude Measurement

After a thorough survey of literature, the investigator identified the following tools on scientific attitude which were found to be useful primarily. They include Baumel and Berger, Kozlow and Nay, Billech and Zakhiriadas, Ravindranath, et al., and Sood and Sanadhya. The specialists in the field of science education were consulted before finalizing the test. The former three tests on scientific attitude were developed in abroad considering their needs and capabilities. Among the tools developed in India, the Scientific Attitude Scale developed by J. K. Sood and R.P. Sanadhya was found most suitable for the present study.

The Scientific Attitude Scale (SAS), thus selected, was subjected to pre-testing, which is, in fact, a 'dress rehearsal' of the final study. The SAS was administered to a sample of hundred tenth class pupils of secondary schools. The validity of the SAS was found 0.83. As these two results were too close to the test results, this Scientific Attitude Scale of J. K. Sood and R. P. Sanadhya was finalised for the final administration to measure the scientific attitude of secondary school pupils. The particulars of the Scientific Attitude Scale in detail are presented herewith.

Scientific Attitude Scale

Scientific Attitude Scale (Appendix-A) was standardized by Dr. J. K. Sood and R. P. Sanadhya.

Dimensions of SAS

The Scientific Attitude Scale consists of six dimensions based on the instrument developed by Billech and Zakhariadas (1975), which consisted of six dimensions, viz., rationality, open-mindedness, curiosity, aversion to superstitions, objectivity of intellectual beliefs and suspended judgement.

Dimension I : Rationality

a) Commitment of the value of rationality.

b) Tendency of test traditional beliefs.

c) Seeking for natural cause of events and identification of cause and effect relationship.

d) Acceptance of criticalness.

e) Challenge of authority.

Dimension II : Curiosity

a) Desire for understanding new situations that are not explained by the existing body of knowledge.

b) Seeking to find out the 'why' and 'how' of observed phenomena.

c) Giving emphasis on the question in approach for novel situation.

d) Desire for completeness of knowledge.

Dimension III : Open-mindedness

a) Willingness to revise opinions and conclusions.

b) Desire for new things and ideas.

c) Rejection of singular and rigid approach to people, things and ideas.

Dimension IV : Aversion to superstitions

a) Rejection of superstitions and false beliefs.

b) Acceptance of scientific facts and explanation.

Dimension V : Objectivity of Intellectual Beliefs

a) Demonstration of the greatest possible concern for observing and recording facts without any influence of personal pride, bias or ambition.

b) Not allowing any change in interpreting results on the basis of present social, economic or political influences.

Dimension VI : Suspended Judgement

a) Unwillingness to draw inferences before evidence is collected.

b) Unwillingness to accept facts that are not supported by the convincing proof.

c) Avoidance of quick judgement.

This Scientific Attitude Scale was constructed by following the Likert Method considering its advantages over other methods. This scale was prepared, based on the contributions made by J. J. Schwab, J. S. Burner, Bertrand Russel, William D. Romey, P. L. Gordner, Victor Y. Billech, Paul B. Diederich, Curtis, Noll, Haney E. Richard, etc.

Item Writing, Editing and Revision

An initial pool of 130 statements was prepared. This pool of statements was given to 10 experienced and qualified educators, after getting its language pruned by experts. The experts were requested to rate each statement on three categories by answering the under mentioned question.

Is the attitude/view measured by this item

- essential
- useful but not essential; or
- not necessary

After collecting the experts' opinions on every statement, content validity ratios (C. V. R.) were calculated. Statements whose CVRs were more than or equal to 0.62 was significant at 0.05 level of significance for N = 10. In this way, the content validity of statements was ascertained quantitatively by utilizing Laushe's (1975) suggestion. Thus out of 130 statements, only 66 were retained for initial tryout.

Initial Tryout

Sixty six statements of different dimensions of scientific attitude were arranged in Likert Method. Fifty percent items were of positive polarity and remaining fifty per cent were of negative polarity. This instrument was administered on a sample and was asked to assign any one of the five following categories after reading each statement carefully.

The five categories were—

SA	Strongly agree
A	Agree
N	Neutral
D	Disagree
SD	Strongly disagree

After the administration of instrument, it was scored by keeping into consideration the scoring procedure suggested by Likert.

For	SA	response	5 scores
	A	response	4
	N	response	3
	D	response	2
	SD	response	1 score

For items of negative polarity, the scoring system was reversed. The t value for 66 statements were calculated to construct a final Scientific Attitude Scale.

Final Form of the Scale

The final form of the Scientific Attitude Scale contained 36 statements of which 18 were of positive polarity and 18 were of negative polarity. The distribution of items were as follows :

Dimension	*Negative Polarity (Item Numbers)*	*Positive Polarity (Item Numbers)*
1. Rationality	1, 2, 6	3, 4 5
2. Curiosity	8, 9	7, 10, 11, 12
3. Open-mindedness	13, 14	15, 16, 17, 18
4. Aversion to superstitions	19, 21, 24	20, 22, 23
5. Objectivity of Intellectual beliefs	25, 26, 28, 30	27, 29
6. Suspended Judgement	31, 32, 34, 35	33, 36

Item Examples of the Scale

Dimension I : Rationality

Positive Item : An idea should not be accepted it is proved to be poor.

SA A N D SD

Negative Item : The ideas are true if few facts support them.

SA A N D SD

Dimension II : Curiosity

Positive Item : Science students should be eager to conduct new experiments.

SA A N D SD

Negative Item : After observing the astonishing situations like magic, a person should not strive to know the secret of it.

SA A N D SD

Dimension III : Open-mindedness

Positive Item : The 'Scientist B' should modify his erroneous concepts if 'Scientist A' presents the correct and fully tested facts before him.

SA A N D SD

Negative Item : One scientist should not give the right to another scientist to defy his established law.

SA A N D SD

Dimension IV : Aversion to superstitions

Positive Item : For weather predictions, magicians and astrologers should not be consulted.

SA A N D SD

Negative Item : It is impossible to defy widely held assumption is society since very long time.

SA A N D SD

Dimension V : Objectivity of Intellectual beliefs

Positive Item : Enough evidence supporting a certain idea should be provided before the idea is accepted.

SA A N D SD

Negative Item : Unacceptable new idea by all people shall not be given due consideration.

SA A N D SD

Dimension VI : Suspended Judgement

Positive Item : If a science teacher fails to arrive at the expected results during demonstration, he should try to discuss the possible causes of its failure.

SA A N D SD

Negative Item : Knowledge once accepted should not be put to test.

SA A N D SD

Scoring Procedure

The scoring procedure for the items of positive polarity is as follows

For	SA	response	5 scores
	A	response	4
	N	response	3
	D	response	2
	SD	response	1 scores

The scoring procedure for the items of negative polarity is as follows

For	SA	response	1 score
	A	response	2
	N	response	3
	D	response	4
	SD	response	5 scores

The maximum and the minimum score of Scientific Attitude Scale is 180 and 36 respectively.

Internal Consistency and Discriminate Validity

The reliability of Scientific Attitude Scale score as calculated by split-half method was found to be 0.88. Scientific Attitude Scale was administered on a sample of 200 and this analysis provided information about the internal consistency and discriminant validity of the six dimensions of the scale. The results are summarized in the following table.

Dimension	*No. of items*	*Relia-bility*	*Internal correlation co-efficient* I	II	III	IV	V	VI
1. Rationality	6	0.76	1.0	0.35	0.31	0.34	0.33	0.32
2. Curiosity	6	0.86	3.5	1.0	5.3	4.8	0.5	0.53
3. Open-mindedness	6	0.84	3.1	0.53	1.0	0.53	0.49	0.53
4. Aversion to superstitions	6	0.80	0.34	0.48	0.53	0.49	0.57	0.53
5. Objectivity of Intellectual beliefs	6	0.73	0.33	0.5	0.49	0.57	1.0	0.53
6. Suspended Judgement	6	0.82	0.32	0.5	0.53	0.53	0.63	1.0
7. Scientific Attitude Scale (Total)	36	0.86	0.62	0.76	0.8	0.81	0.85	0.82

Reliability coefficient for six dimensions of Scientific Attitude Scale were found to be 0.76, 0.86, 0.84, 0.80, 0.73, and 0.82 respectively. These high coefficients reflect the strength of each dimension for measuring the scientific attitude. In addition to this, high correlation coefficients between the total scientific attitude scores on various dimensions taken separately to justify the inclusion of these dimenstion in the scale. From the above table it is evident that the correlation coefficients were found to be 0.62, 0.76, 0.80, 0.81, 0.85, and 0.82 respectively.

Scientific Aptitude Measurement

Scientific Aptitude Test was then taken into consideration for finalization. A review of the scientific aptitude tests revealed that there were tests developed by Verma, Mitra, Chaudari, Deshpande, Mukherji and Chatterji, Gupta, Ohja, Sharma, Agarwal and Nair, *et al.*

Out of these tests available on scientific aptitude, the Kerala University Science Aptitude Test of Nair, *et al.*, was selected for the use in the present study, which is in active use till to-date in University of Kerala and University of Calicut. This test was also administered to a sample of 100 tenth class pupils studying in secondary schools to pre-test its usefulness. The reliability was found to be nearest to the test reliability, and hence this Kerala University Science Aptitude Test was selected for final use to measure the scientific aptitude of secondary school pupils. The details of the Science Aptitude Test are given herewith.

Kerala University Science Aptitude Test

The Kerala University Science Aptitude Test (Appendix-B) standardized by Nair, A. S., R. Ramanandan, and N. P. Pillai was selected for collection of data regarding science aptitude of secondary school pupils. The details regarding the test are given below.

Test Components

The test consists of five sub-tests, viz., Number Series, Science Information, Formulation, Spatial Ability and Verbal Comprehension and Interpretation. The components of the test, number of items and time allotted for each sub-test are given below.

No. of Sub-tests	*Name of Sub-tests*	*No. of Items*	*Time in minutes*	*Weight assigned to each item*
I	Number Series	24	15	15/24
II	Science Information	20	5	5/20
III	Formulation	10	8	8/10
IV	Spatial Ability	20	16	16/20
V	Verbal Comprehension and Interpretation	16	18	18/16

1. Number Series

Numbers are arranged in a particular sequence in the following lines. In each line one or more numbers are omitted. Such places are shown with "------------" (blanks). Moreover, the last blank in each line is shown separately with a + mark.

Read the numbers in each line and understand the sequence and find out the number to be placed in the place of X. On the right side against the line answers are given under A, B, C, D, E groups. From these choices sample has 16 find out the correct answer and to make a + mark in the appropriate circle of the answer sheet.

Example	Choices A B C D E	Answer Sheet A B C D E
1. 2 3 4 5 6 .....8 X	6 7 8 9 10	O O O O ⊕
2. 16 14 12 10 ....64 X	8 5 3 1 2	⊕ O O O O

2. Science Information

Read the following each statement and decide whether they are right or wrong. If it is right make a + mark in the circle below T (True) in the answer sheet indicating the number of the statement. If it is wrong, make + mark in the circle below F (False).

Example **Answer Sheet**

	T	F
A. Iron is a metal	⊕	O
B. Magnet does not attract iron.	O	⊕

3. Formulation

In this test there are 10 simple arithmetic problems. Work out the problem mentally. Under each question there are five answers. Find out the correct one and make a + mark in the appropriate place in the answer sheet.

Example **Answer Sheet**

	A	B	C	D	E
1. If 5X = 10, what is the value of X ? (A) 10 (B) 5 (C) 2 (D) 15 (E) 3	O	O	⊕	O	O
1. If X and Y are two numbers, what is total ? (A)X+Y (B) XY (C) X–Y (D) Y (E) 2XY	⊕	O	O	O	O

4. Spatial Ability

Each test item consists of a picture. Six answers are given for each item. Pupils have to find out which pictures are the correct ones, when the first one is rotated to the right or left side, and they have to mark the response in the answer sheet. There may be 2 or 3 correct answers for each item. An example is given below:

5. Verbal Comprehension and Interpretation

Here a few paragraphs, and under each of them selected questions or incomplete statements together with their answers are given. Pupils have to read the paragraphs, find out the correct answers and mark them in the response sheet. An examples is given below.

Digestion takes place to a great extent in the stomach. The gastric juice that is secreted by the cells of the stomach wall contains an enzyme called pepsin and hydrochloric acid. pH level conducive for the digestion of protein is supplied to pepsin by hydrochloric acid.

Here arises an interesting problem. Though the gastric juice is a powerful liquid which has the ability to digest protein, why does not digest the stomach wall which is made up of (mainly) protein. So far nothing much is known about it. However certain cells in the stomach wall produce a mucous substance and this substance covers the whole stomach wall and protects the cells of the stomach wall. Experiencing strong emotions like fear and anger at the time of taking food will prevent the production of mucous substance. Unfortunately, when the self-protecting devices of the stomach fail to function, the stomach wall also occasionally undergoes digestion and the ulcers result.

1. pH required for protein digestion is obtained from

   A. food B. air

   C. gastric juice D. none of the above

2. The protein digesting juice is not digesting the stomach wall which is mainly made up of protein. The reason is

   A. Due to some inactivity of the protein digesting juice to the protein of the stomach wall.

   B. An obstacle prevents to have contact with the protein of stomach.

   C. The protein digesting juice has the ability to digest only the protein in the food and not any other proteins.

   D. The protein of the stomach wall is so powerful that protein digesting juice can not digest it.

   E. None of the above.

3. The shortage of what secretion causes ulcer

   A. The mucous of stomach B. The HCl in the stomach

   C. Enzymes in the gastric juice D. Pepsin of the gastric juice

   E. None of the above.

4. When we are with high emotions, change in the rate of digestion will

   A. Remain same B. Increase C. Decrease

   D. Depend on the nature of emotions

   E. Neither increase nor decrease

Validity and Reliability of the Test

Validity of the test was ensured mainly by adopting components from other tests of proved merit and partly by ensuring high internal validity attained through item analysis. Further the inter-correlations of the five tests in the battery show high relation among different components.

Predictive value of this test was calculated by correlating the scores in the test with school achievement as an extend criterion. The validity coefficient came to be 0.504.

The split-half reliability was worked out for the whole test battery as well as the component test and corrected for shortening using the Spearman-Brown formula. The reliability coefficients of this test are given below.

No.	*Name of Sub-test*	*Reliability coefficients*
1.	Number series	0.81
2.	Science information	0.60
3.	Formulation	0.50
4.	Spatial Ability	0.91
5.	Verbal Comprehension and Interpretation	0.55
6.	Whole test	0.88

The test-retest reliability of the whole test was also calculated using conventional methods. The coefficient of reliability came to 0.78.

Scoring Scheme

One score is given to each correct answer and zero to incorrect answer. The total of these marks is taken and is considered as the score of science aptitude of each subject. The maximum and minimum score of the Aptitude Test are 80 and 0.

The tools, viz., Scientific Attitude Scale of J. K. Sood and R. P. Sanadhya and Kerala University Science Aptitude Test of Nair, et al. were finalized and used for the collection of data.

4

Data Analysis

The next steps in the process of research, after the collection of data, are the organization, analysis and interpretation of data and formulation of conclusions and generalizations to get a meaningful picture out of the raw information collected. The analysis and interpretation of data involve the objective material in the possession of the researcher and his subjective reactions and desires to be derived from the data the inherent meaning in their relation to the problem.

The mass data collected through the use of various tools, need to be systematized and organized i.e., edited, classified and tabulated before it can serve the purpose. Here, editing implies the checking of gathered data for accuracy, utility and completeness; classifying refers to the dividing of the information into different categories, classes or heads, for use; and tabulating denotes the recording of the classified material in accurate mathematical terms,. e.g., marking and counting frequency tallies for different items on which information is gathered.

Analysis of data means studying the tabulated material in order to determine inherent facts or meanings. It involves breaking down the existing complex factors into simpler parts and putting the parts together in new arrangements for purposes of interpretation.

This present chapter, Analysis of Data, hence includes a study of the different techniques adopted for analysis and interpretation of data, and the results that resulted from the analysis of data.

After finalizing the tools and sample for the study, the data were collected from six hundred pupils studying in tenth class. Scientific Attitude Scale of J.K. Sood and R.P. Sanadhya was used to identify the scientific attitude possessed by the sample, the Kerala University Science Aptitude Test of Nair, et al. was employed to study the level of scientific aptitude possessed by the tenth class pupils. After the collection of data was finished, it was analysed keeping the objectives and hypotheses of the study in view. The analysis of data was carried out in the following manner.

As mentioned earlier in the previous chapters, the study includes three major aspects, viz., scientific attitude, scientific aptitude, and the association between these two. From the tools, the total scores of scientific attitude and scientific aptitude were taken as raw scores for each candidate. This raw data were put to statistical treatment. Each of the different aspects, viz., scientific attitude and scientific aptitude of the study was taken first into consideration individually. Latter these aspects were tested for their interrelationship. The hypotheses framed were statistically tested and accordingly accepted or rejected.

SCIENTIFIC ATTITUDE

The total score of scientific attitude of each pupil was taken to find out the level of scientific attitude possessed by each sub-sample as well as total sample of the study. The maximum score that a pupil can get is 180 and the minimum is 36. In the present study, the highest score secured by a pupil was 161 and the lowest was 87.

For the purpose of classification of the level of scientific attitude possessed by the sample, the scientific attitude level was categorized by using the normal probability of distribution. the pupil who scored 114 and below was kept in low scientific attitude group, who scored between 115 and 149 was put in average scientific attitude group, and who scored 150 and above was placed in high scientific attitude group.

The mean scores were used to identify the level of scientific attitude possessed by the pupils and to compare the sub-sample variation. The values of standard deviation were used 'to measure the spread or dispersion of scores in a distribution. The null hypotheses formulated for this study were accordingly accepted or rejected. The critical ratios were calculated to test the significant difference in the means of the two sub-samples of each variable.

The chi-square (X^2) test of independence was applied for 'comparing the experimentally obtained results with those of to be expected theoretically on some hypothesis'.

Hypothesis 1 : Secondary School Pupil will Possess High Scientific Attitude.

To test the validity of Hypothesis, 1, the total scores of all the sample were calculated to arrive at mean, and standard deviation of the sample. The results are as follows.

Table 4.1 : Level of Scientific Attitude Possessed by the Whole Sample

Sample	*Mean*	*Standard Deviation*
600	131.53	17.97

The pupils studying in secondary schools hold average level of scientific attitude. In the sample, as per the standard deviation, there is a little bit of higher dispersion of scores in the units of the sample.

the chi-square (x^2) test of independence was applied to test the divergence of observed results from those expected on the hypothesis of equal probability of distribution of a trait in the sample.

Table 4.2 : Distribution of Scientific Attitude in the Whole Sample

Sample		*Low*	*Average*	*High*	x^2
600	f_o	86	419	95	1.35*
	f_e	96	408	96	

df = 2 P at 0.01 level is 9.21 * Not significant at 0.01 level

f_o= frequency of occurrence of observed or experimentally determined facts

f_e= frequency of occurrence expected on some hypothesis

It is clear, from Table 4.2, that the distribution of scientific attitude in the whole population is normal.

The hypothesis ***that the secondary school pupils will possess high scientific attitude*** can be rejected as the pupils hold an average scientific attitude.

Hypothesis 1 A : There is no significant difference in the level of scientific attitude possessed by boys and girls of secondary schools.

A comparison of the scientific attitude scores of boys and girls was made to find out the difference in the level of scientific attitude possessed by them. The data are as follows.

Table 4.3 : Comparison of Scientific Attitude of Boys and Girls

Variable	*Sample*	*Mean*	*Standard deviation*	*Mean difference*	*Critical ratio*
Boys	300	129.29	23.67		
				1.45	0.85*
Girls	300	130.74	18.39		

P at 0.01 level is 2.58   * Not significant at 0.01 level

From Table 4.3, it can be seen that boys and girls of secondary schools hold average scientific attitude. It can also be seen clearly that there is no significant difference in the level of scientific attitude possessed by both boys and girls as there is no significant difference in the mean scores of both cases. But the standard deviation indicates that the divergence in scores is more in boys than in girls.

As the critical ratio value is not significant, it can be said that the little difference that exists may be due to sampling error.

Further, the chi-square test was applied to test the divergence of observed results of boys and girls from those expected on the hypothesis of equal probability. The chi-square values were calculated for each sub-sample and are given below in Table 4.4.

Table 4.4 : Distribution of Scientific Attitude in Boys and Girls

Variable	*Sample*		*Low*	*Average*	*High*	X^2	*Skewness trend*
		f_o	43	212	45		
Boys	300					1.02*	Normal
		f_e	48	204	48		
		f_o	43	207	50		
Girls	300					0.65*	Normal
		f_e	48	204	48		

df = 2   P at 0.01 level is 9.21   * Not significant at 0.01 level

As can be seen from the above Table, it can be concluded that the scientific attitude is distributed normally in both boys and girls as the chi-square values are not significant.

The hypothesis *that there is no significant difference in the level of scientific attitude possessed by boys and girls of secondary schools* can be accepted.

Hypothesis 1 B : There is no significant difference in scientific attitude possessed by the pupils of private and government secondary schools.

To test the validity of Hypothesis 1 B, a comparison of the scientific attitude scores was made. The values are given below.

Table 4.5 : Comparison of Scientific Attitude of the Pupils of Private and Government Schools

Variable	*Sample*	*Mean*	*Standard deviation*	*Mean difference*	*Critical ratio*
Private Schools	300	133.32	15.17	4.09	2.74*
Govt. Schools	300	129.23	20.82		

P at 0.01 level is 2.58 * Not significant at 0.01 level

The above Table states that there is a significant difference between the mean scores of the pupils studying in private and government secondary schools. The pupils of private schools hold higher scientific attitude than those of government schools, but both the groups hold an average level of scientific attitude.

The critical ratio value also states that there is significant difference in the level of scientific attitude possessed by the pupils of private and government schools.

The chi-square test was applied to test the divergence of observed results from those expected. The results are presented on p. 76.

There is a significant difference in the level of scientific attitude possessed by the pupils of both private and government schools. The chi-square value is more significant in the case of private schools than that of government schools indicating that there is a greater divergence in the distribution of scientific attitude in the pupils of private schools.

The skewness trend indicates that the scientific attitude tends towards high in the pupils of private schools and towards low in the pupils of government schools.

Table 4.6 : Distribution of Scientific Attitude in the Pupils of Private and Government Schools

Variable	*Sample*		*Low*	*Average*	*High*	*X²*	*Skewness trend*
Private	300	f_o	16	244	40	30.5*	→
		f_e	48	204	48		
Government	300	f_o	70	175	55	15.2*	←
		f_e	48	204	48		

* Significant at 0.01 level

The hypothesis ***that there is no significant difference in the level of scientific attitude possessed by the pupils of private and government schools*** can be rejected.

Hypothesis 1 C : There is no significant difference in the level of scientific attitude possessed by the pupils of rural and urban secondary schools.

A comparison was made to identify the difference in the possession of scientific attitude by the pupils residing in urban and rural areas. The results are as follows.

Table 4.7 : Comparison of Scientific Attitude of the Pupils of Urban and Rural Schools

Variable	*Sample*	*Mean*	*Standard deviation*	*Mean difference*	*Critical ratio*
Urban Schools	300	127.8	17.97	7.53	5.41*
Rural Schools	300	135.33	16.07		

* Significant at 0.01 level

As can be seen from Table 4.7, there is a significant difference in the level of scientific attitude possessed by the tenth class pupils residing in rural and urban areas. The pupils studying in rural schools hold higher scientific attitude than those of urban schools, but both the groups fall under average scientific attitude category.

The value of critical ration states that there is high significance in the difference of scientific attitude possessed by both the samples.

The chi-square test values of the pupils studying in rural schools and urban school are as follows.

Table 4.8 : Distribution of Scientific Attitude in the Pupils of Urban and Rural Schools

Variable	*Sample*		*Low*	*Average*	*High*	X^2	*Skewness trend*
		f_o	53	208	39		
Urban	300					2.28*	Nor-
		f_e	48	204	48		mal
		f_o	33	211	56		
Rural	300					6.26*	Nor-
		f_e	48	204	48		mal

* Not Significant at 0.01 level

From the above Table 4.8, it is clear that the distribution of scientific attitude in various levels is normal, as both the chi-square values are significant. However, the pupils of urban schools slightly tend towards low scientific attitude as against the rural sample.

It can be said, from the data of Table 4.7 and 4.8, even though there is a significant difference in the levei of scientific attitude possessed by the pupils of rural and urban areas, the distribution of it is normal in both the cases.

The hypothesis *that there is no significant difference in the level of scientific attitude possessed by the pupils of rural and urban secondary schools* can be rejected.

Hypothesis 1 D : There is no significant difference in the level of scientific attitude possessed by the pupil of English and Telugu medium secondary schools.

A comparison was made between the pupils studying telugu medium schools an those studying in English medium schools regarding the scientific attitude scores to test the validity of hypothesis 1 D. The details are as shown on p. 78.

There is, according to Table 4.9, a significant difference in the level of scientific attitude possessed by the pupils studying in English medium and Telugu medium schools. The pupils of English medium hold high scientific attitude. But, both the samples possess an average level of scientific attitude.

Table 4.9 : Comparison of Scientific Attitude of the Pupils of Telugu and English Medium Schools

Variable	*Sample*	*Mean*	*Standard deviation*	*Mean difference*	*Critical ratio*
Telugu	480	130.59	18.22	4.91	3.38*
English	120	135.5	13.01		

* Significant at 0.01 level

Further, chi-square test of independence was applied to measure the divergence of results in both the samples. The data are given herewith.

Table 4.10 : Distribution of Scientific Attitude in the Pupils of Telugu Medium and English Medium Schools

Variable	*Sample*		*Low*	*Average*	*High*	X^2	*Skewness trend*
Telugu	480	f_o	81	333	66	1.88*	Normal
		f_e	76.8	324.4	76.8		
English	120	f_o	5	86	29	15.74**	→
		f_e	19.2	81.6	19.2		

* Not Significant at 0.01 level ** Significant at 0.01 level

From Table 4.10, it seems that there is a significant divergence in the observed results in the pupils studying in English medium as the chi-square value is high in this case. The skewness trend in the English medium schools is towards high Scientific attitude.

The hypothesis ***that there is no significant difference in the level of scientific attitude possessed by the pupils of English and Telugu medium secondary school pupil*** **can be rejected.**

Hypothesis 1 E : There is no significant difference in the level of scientific attitude possessed by the pupils of residential and non-residential secondary schools.

To test the difference in the level of scientific attitude possessed, if exists, by the pupils of residential and non-residential schools, a comparison was made. The results are as follows.

Table 4.11 : Comparison of Scientific Attitude of the Pupils of Residential and Non-residential Schools

Variable	*Sample*	*Mean*	*Standard deviation*	*Mean difference*	*Critical ratio*
Residential	120	140.68	15.98	12.19	7.12*
Non-Residential	480	128.49	19.42		

* Significant at 0.01 level

There is a high significant difference in the level of scientific attitude possessed by the pupils of residential by the pupils of residential and non-residential schools. The pupils of residential schools hold high average scientific attitude. The value of critical ration also states that there is a high level significance in the difference of the level of scientific attitude possessed by both the samples.

It is, further, tried to test the divergence of the results of the pupils of residential and non-residential schools. Chi-square test of independence was calculated for both the samples, which are given below.

Table 4.12 : Distribution of Scientific Attitude in the Pupils of Residential and Non-residential Schools

Variable	*Sample*		*Low*	*Average*	*High*	*X^2*	*Skewness trend*
Residential	120	f_o	81	73	39	15.74*	→
		f_e	19.2	81.6	19.2		
Non-residential	480	f_o	78	78	346	6.83**	Normal
		f_e	76.8	76.8	326.4		

** Not Significant at 0.01 level * Significant at 0.01 level

The divergence in the distribution of scientific attitude, according to Table 4.12, is seen only in the pupils of residential schools as the chi-square value is highly significant. The skewness trend in the above in the above sample is towards the high scientific attitude level in the pupils of residential schools, but the scientific attitude in the pupils of non-residential schools is distributed normally.

The hypothesis *that there is no significant difference in the level of scientific attitude possessed by the pupils of residential and non-residential secondary school* can be rejected.

SCIENTIFIC APTITUDE

To measure the level of scientific aptitude possessed by each sub-sample as well as whole sample of the study, the total score of scientific aptitude of each pupil was taken into consideration. The maximum score that a pupil can get is 80 and the minimum is O. In the present study, the highest score secured was 61 and the lowest was 11.

For the purpose of classification of scientific aptitude possessed by the samples, the scientific aptitude level was categorized by applying the normal probability of distribution. The pupil who scored 19 and below was kept in low scientific aptitude group, and the pupil who scored 40 and above was placed in high scientific aptitude group.

The mean scores were utilized to compare the sub-sample variation. The values of standard deviation were used to measure the dispersion of scores in each case. The chi-square test of independence was used for computing the experimentally obtained results with those to be expected theoretical on a hypothesis. Accordingly the null hypothesis framed for this study was accepted or rejected.

Hypothesis 2 : Secondary School pupils will possess high scientific aptitude

The validity of Hypotheses 2 was tested by calculating mean, standard deviation and chi-square values. The results are as follows.

Table 4.13 : Level of Scientific Aptitude Possessed by the Whole Sample

Sample	*Mean*	*Standard Deviation*
600	29.56	10.23

It is evident, from Table 4.13, that the pupils of secondary schools hold average level of scientific aptitude.

The chi-square test of independence was applied to identify the divergence in the dispersion of scientific aptitude in the sample.

Table 4.14 : Distribution of Scientific Aptitude in the Whole Sample

Sample		*Low*	*Average*	*High*	x^2
600	f_o	99	401	100	0.38*
	f_e	96	408	96	

df = 2 P at 0.01 level is 9.21 * Not significant at 0.01 level

As per the chi-square value, the distribution of scientific aptitude in the sample is supporting the assumption that any psychological trait will distribute normally.

The hypothesis *that secondary school pupils will possess high scientific aptitude* can be rejected, as the pupils possess an average scientific aptitude.

Hypothesis 2 A : There is no significant difference in the level of scientific aptitude possessed by boys and girls of secondary schools.

The data of the sub-samples were computed to test the validity of the above hypothesis. The calculations are as follows.

Table 4.15 : Comparison of Scientific Aptitude of Boys and Girls

Variable	*Sample*	*Mean*	*Standard deviation*	*Mean difference*	*Critical ratio*
Boys	300	30.33	10.26		
				1.09	1.28*
Girls	300	29.24	10.56		

P at 0.01 level is 2.58   * Not significant at 0.01 level

From the mean scores of table 4.15, it is clear that there is no significant difference between the level of scientific aptitude possessed by both boys and girls. this is supported by the value of critical ratio. Both the sub-samples are with average scientific aptitude.

It is further tried to identify the distribution of scientific aptitude in the sub-samples.

Table 4.16 : Distribution of Scientific Aptitude in Boys and Girls

Variable	*Sample*		*Low*	*Average*	*High*	*X^2*	*Skewness trend*
		f_o	36	215	49		
Boys	300					3.6*	Normal
		f_e	48	204	48		
		f_o	36	215	49		
Girls	300					3.6*	Normal
		f_e	48	204	48		

df = 2   P at 0.01 level is 9.21   * Not significant at 0.01 level

The chi-square values, according to Table 16, of both boys and girls are not significant. So the distribution of scientific aptitude in the sub-samples is normal.

The hypothesis *that there is no significant difference in the level of scientific aptitude possessed by boys and girls of secondary schools* can be accepted.

Hypothesis 2 B : There is no significant difference in the level of scientific aptitude possessed by the pupils of private and government secondary schools.

The validity of Hypothesis 2 B was tested by computing necessary calculations. They are as follows.

Table 4.17 : Comparison of Scientific Aptitude of the Pupils of Private and Government Schools

Variable	*Sample*	*Mean*	*Standard deviation*	*Mean difference*	*Critical ratio*
Private Schools	300	32.52	11.14	5.54	5.75*
Govt. Schools	300	26.98	8.95		

* Significant at 0.01 level

It is evident, from Table 4.17, that there is a significant difference in the level of scientific aptitude possessed by the pupils studying in private and government schools. The pupils studying in private schools hold high scientific aptitude than those of government schools, but both the sub-samples are with average scientific aptitude.

Further, the chi-square test was applied to identify the distribution of scientific aptitude in the sub-samples.

Table 4.18 : Distribution of Scientific Aptitude in the Pupils of Private and Government Schools

Variable	*Sample*		*Low*	*Average*	*High*	*X^2*	*Skewness trend*
Private	300	f_o	41	184	75	18.17*	→
		f_e	48	204	48		
Government	300	f_o	50	217	25	13.93*	←
		f_e	48	204	48		

* Significant at 0.01 level

The distribution of scientific aptitude, according to Table 4.18, is not normal in both the pupils studying in private and government schools, as the chi-square values are significant. The skewness trend is towards high scientific aptitude in the case of pupils studying in private schools, whereas it is towards low scientific aptitude in the pupils of government schools.

The hypothesis *that there is no significant difference in the level of scientific aptitude possessed by the pupil of private and government schools* can be rejected.

Hypothesis 2 C : There is no significant difference in the level of scientific aptitude possessed by the pupils of urban and rural secondary schools.

The validity of Hypothesis 2 C was tested in the following manner.

Table 4.19 : Comparison of Scientific Aptitude of the Pupils of Urban and Rural Schools

Variable	*Sample*	*Mean*	*Standard deviation*	*Mean difference*	*Critical ratio*
Urban	300	32.01	11.46	4.37	5.32*
Rural	300	27.64	8.44		

* Significant at 0.01 level

There is a difference in the level of scientific aptitude possessed by the pupils studying in urban and rural schools as per the mean score values of the sub-samples. The urban pupils are relatively better in holding scientific aptitude than the rural pupils.

It is, further, tried to know the skewness trend of the distribution of scientific aptitude in the sub-samples.

Table 4.20 : Distribution of Scientific Aptitude in the Pupils of Urban and Rural Schools

Variable	*Sample*		*Low*	*Average*	*High*	*X^2*	*Skewness trend*
Urban	300	f_o	54	168	78	25.85*	→
		f_e	48	204	48		
Rural	300	f_o	45	233	22	18.39*	←
		f_e	48	204	48		

* Significant at 0.01 level

The distribution of scientific aptitude in the pupils studying in urban and rural schools is not normal as the chi-square values are highly significant. The skewness trend is very high towards high scientific aptitude in urban sample. But, the skewness trend of distribution of scientific aptitude in rural sample is towards low scientific aptitude.

The hypothesis ***that there is no significant difference in the level of scientific aptitude possessed by the pupils of urban and rural schools*** can be rejected.

Hypothesis 2 D : There is no significant difference in the level of scientific aptitude possessed by the pupils of Telugu and English medium secondary schools.

The Hypothesis 2 D was tested for its validity by comparing the scores of the sub-samples.

Table 4.21 : Comparison of Scientific Aptitude of the Pupils of Telugu and English Medium Schools

Variable	*Sample*	*Mean*	*Standard deviation*	*Mean difference*	*Critical ratio*
Telugu	480	37.00	15.47	3.72	3.15*
English	120	40.72	10.37		

* Significant at 0.01 level

The means scores of Telugu medium and English medium pupils say that there is a difference in the level of scientific aptitude in the two groups. The English medium pupils hold slightly high scientific aptitude than the Telugu medium pupils. But, both the samples are with average scientific aptitude. The critical ration value also makes the difference significant.

Table 4.22 : Distribution of Scientific Aptitude in the Pupils of Telugu Medium and English Medium Schools

Variable	*Sample*		*Low*	*Average*	*High*	X^2	*Skewness trend*
Telugu	480	f_o	96	352	32	32.9*	→
		f_e	76.8	326.4	76.8		
English	120	f_o	3	56	61	112.7*	→
		f_e	19.2	81.6	19.2		

* Significant at 0.01 level

As the difference is found significant in the sub-samples, it is further put to the chi-square test to identify the distribution of scientific aptitude in the two groups.

It is clear, from Table 4.22, that the distribution of scientific aptitude of the pupils of Telugu medium and English medium is no normal. The skewness trend in English medium pupils is very high towards high scientific aptitude. But the trend is towards low in the case of Telugu medium pupils

The hypothesis *that there is no significant difference in the level of scientific aptitude possessed by the pupils of Telugu and English medium pupils* can be rejected.

Hypothesis 2 E : There is no significant difference in the level of scientific aptitude possessed by the pupils of residential and non-residential secondary schools.

The Hypothesis 2 E was tested for its validity by calculating mean, standard deviation and critical ratio values. The data are as follows.

Table 4.23 : Comparison of Scientific Attitude of the Pupils of Residential and Non-residential Schools

Variable	*Sample*	*Mean*	*Standard deviation*	*Mean difference*	*Critical ratio*
Residential	120	32.73	10.23	3.73	3.58*
Non-Residential	480	29.00	10.42		

* Significant at 0.01 level

The mean scores, in Table 4.23, indicate that there is a difference in the level of scientific aptitude possessed by the pupils of residential and non-residential schools. The pupils of residential schools hold a little bit higher scientific aptitude than those of non-residential schools.

As the difference in the two groups is significant, it is tried to test the distribution of scientific aptitude in the samples as shown on p.86.

The results indicates that the scientific aptitude in the two groups is differently distributed. The scientific aptitude in the pupils of residential schools is not normally distributed and the skewness trend is towards high scientific aptitude. Contrary to this, the scientific aptitude is distributed normally in the pupils of non-residential schools.

Table 4.24 : Distribution of Scientific Aptitude in the Pupils of Residential and Non-residential Schools

Variable	*Sample*		*Low*	*Average*	*High*	*X²*	*Skewness trend*
		f_o	7	94	19		
Residential	120					9.63*	→
		f_e	19.2	81.6	19.2		
		f_o	92	307	81		
Non-residential	480					4.39**	Normal
		f_e	76.8	326.4	76.8		

** Not Significant at 0.01 level * Significant at 0.01 level

The hypothesis ***that there is no significant difference in the level of scientific aptitude possessed by the pupils of residential and non-residential secondary school pupils*** can be rejected.

ASSOCIATION BETWEEN SCIENTIFIC ATTITUDE AND SCIENTIFIC APTITUDE

The present study is intended to identify whether there exists any association between scientific attitude and scientific aptitude. For this, the values of chi-square test of independence were computed, by which the association among these three areas was to be identified. The statistical data and their results are given below.

Hypothesis 3 : **There will be a significant positive association between scientific attitude and scientific aptitude in secondary school pupils.**

To test the validity of Hypothesis 3, the chi-square values were computed.

Table 4.25 : Association in the Whole Sample (X^2 values)

Sample	*Scientific Attitude with Scientific Aptitude*
600	10.3.58*

df = 2 P at 0.01 level is 9.21 * Significant at 0.01 level

The chi-square values indicate that there is a great association between scientific attitude and scientific aptitude.

The hypothesis ***that there will be a significant positive association between scientific attitude and scientific aptitude secondary school pupils*** can be accepted.

Hypothesis 3 A : There is no significant positive association between scientific attitude and scientific aptitude of boys and girls of secondary schools.

The association between scientific attitude and scientific aptitude boys and girls was tried in the following way.

Table 4.26 : Association in Boys and Girls (X^2 values)

Variable	*Sample*	*Scientific Attitude with Scientific Aptitude*
Boys	300	99.97*
Girls	300	84.99*

* Significant at 0.01 level

There is a good association between scientific attitude and scientific aptitude of boys and girls. The association is more in boys than in girls.

The hypothesis ***that there is no significant association between scientific attitude and scientific aptitude of boys and girls of secondary schools*** can be rejected.

Hypothesis 3 B : There is no significant positive association between scientific attitude and scientific aptitude of the pupils of private and government secondary schools.

To test the validity of Hypothesis 3 B, the chi-square values computed.

Table 4.27 : Association in the Pupils of Private and Government Schools (X^2 values)

Variable	*Sample*	*Scientific Attitude with Scientific Aptitude*
Private	300	407.12*
Govt.	300	105.76*

* Significant at 0.01 level

There is a significant positive association between scientific attitude and scientific aptitude. The association is more in private schools than in government schools.

The hypothesis ***that there is no significant positive association between scientific attitude and scientific aptitude of the pupils of private and government schools*** **can be rejected.**

Hypotheses 3 C : There is no significant positive association between scientific attitude and scientific aptitude of the pupils of urban and rural secondary schools.

The Hypothesis 3 C was tested for its validity by applying the chi-square test. The results are as follows.

Table 4.28 : Association in the Pupils of Urban and Rural Schools (X^2 values)

Variable	*Sample size*	*Scientific Attitude with Scientific Aptitude*
Urban	300	170.38*
Rural	300	170.39*

* Significant at 0.01 level

There is a significant positive association between scientific attitude and scientific aptitude in the pupils studying in urban and rural schools. The association is more in urban schools than in rural schools.

The hypothesis *that there is no significant positive association between scientific attitude and scientific aptitude in the pupils of rural and urban secondary schools* can be rejected.

Hypothesis 3 D : There is no significant positive association between scientific attitude and scientific aptitude of the pupils of Telugu and English medium secondary schools.

The chi-square test was applied to identify the level of association between scientific attitude and scientific aptitude of the pupils of Telugu and English medium schools. The results are as shown in Table 4.29.

The chi-square values from the Table 4.29 indicate that there is a significant positive association between scientific attitude and scientific aptitude of the pupils of Telugu and English medium schools. The association is more in Telugu medium schools than in English medium schools.

Table 4.29 : Association in the Pupils Studying in Telugu and English Medium Schools (X^2 values)

Variable	*Sample size*	*Scientific Attitude with Scientific Aptitude*
Telugu	480	99.28*
English	120	29.26*

* Significant at 0.01 level

The hypothesis ***that there is no significant positive association between scientific attitude and scientific aptitude of the pupils of Telugu and English medium secondary schools*** can be rejected.

Hypothesis 3 E : There is no significant positive association between scientific attitude and scientific aptitude of the pupils of residential and non-residential secondary schools.

To test the validity of Hypothesis 3 E, the chi-square values were computed and are given here under.

Table 4.30 : Association in the Pupils of Residential and Non-residentials Schools (X^2 values)

Variable	*Sample size*	*Scientific Attitude with Scientific Aptitude*
Residential	300	24.33*
Non-Residential	300	172.98*

* Significant at 0.01 level

There is a significant positive relationship between scientific attitude and scientific aptitude of the pupils of residential and non-residential schools. The association is very high in non-residential schools.

The hypothesis ***that there is no significant positive association between scientific attitude and scientific aptitude in the pupils of residential and non-residential secondary schools*** can be rejected.

5

Summary, Conclusions, Discussion and Suggestions

We, as the citizens of the present modern world, see the countless manifestations of science all around us. There is no aspect of our life today which has not been influenced by science one way or the other. This is because we live in an age of scientific culture. Science has shrunk the world and totally changed the human outlook. In fact, science now has all-pervading influence on every sphere of human activity. Further, modern science is no longer confined to the surface of this globe, its sphere of achievements reached beyond the earth.

There has been, in recent times, rapid addition of knowledge to the world of science. Great achievements of science and technology and the use of these scientific achievements in promoting the well-being of mankind through their application in the field of industry, communication, transport, engineering, agriculture and medicine have made science more important than ever before. Science, has, in fact, radically transformed the material environment of the citizens of the modern world; and, of course, it has its significant role in promoting culture and spiritualism either directly or indirectly.

Teaching of everyday science for everybody has become an unavoidable part of general education. Nobody questions its inclusion as a subject in the school curriculum. It is included in a school's curriculum for the same reasons as any other subject, but in addition, science inculcates certain special values peculiar to it and which no other subject can provide Besides satisfying the usual needs for its inclusion as a subject in the curriculum- such as intellectual, cultural, moral aesthetic, utilitarian as well as vocational values- science learning provides training in scientific method, and also helps to develop a scientific attitude of mind and scientific aptitude in the learner. Therefore, science is now a compulsory subject in every system of school education right from the elementary level.

Since the beginning of the twentieth century, science educators have included the development of scientific attitude among the general aims of science education. The scientific attitude, by its very name, tends to be associated solely with the area of science. A person who has scientific attitude (1) is open-minded, (2) shows intellectual honesty, (3) suspends judgements until he gets accurate information, (4) looks for cause and effect relationship, (5) listens to others' point of view, (6) is free from superstitions, (7) has a habit of basing judgement on fact, (8) is willing to change opinions on the basis of evidence, (9) is able to distinguish between fact and theory, (10) is curious concerning things, (11) is desirous for experimental verification, and (12) is with rational thinking.

Scientific aptitude is a complex of interacting hereditary and environmental determinants producing predispositions or abilities in science. It is a potentiality for future accomplishment in science without regard to past training and achievement. It appears to be dependent upon a variety of factors such as study skills, motivation, persistence in learning a subject, socio-economic factors, cultural background, interests and attitudes.

Considering their role in determining scientific attitude, scientific aptitude and achievement in biology, variables such as boys versus girls, rural versus urban schools, English versus Telugu medium schools, private versus government schools, and residential versus non-residential schools are selected.

Objectives are identified keeping the different aspects of the present study in view. The main objectives of the study are:

1. To find out the scientific attitude and scientific aptitude possessed by the secondary school pupils.
2. To find out the association among scientific attitude and scientific aptitude of secondary schools pupils.

3. To compare the scientific attitude and scientific aptitude of boys and girls, rural versus urban schools, English versus Telugu medium schools, private versus government schools and residential versus non-residential schools.

Hypotheses are formulated taking the above objectives into consideration. These hypotheses are formulated only in positive manner, but the sub-hypotheses are formulated in Null form. The main hypotheses of the present study are:

1. Secondary school pupils will possess high scientific attitude.
2. Secondary school pupils will possess high scientific aptitude.
3. There will be a significant positive association between scientific attitude, and scientific aptitude.

Stratified sampling technique, after making a detailed study of different techniques of sampling, is found the most appropriate technique for the present study as this study involves splitting of the sample into a good number of groups according to different variables. Through stratified sampling only it is possible to divide the sample into different groups and choose pupils from each of these groups. Random sampling technique is also employed to select pupils from each group.

Regarding the **size of the sample,** 600 is found appropriate. This is found suitable because the study involves due intensity and detail, a sample with more than 600 pupils would involve a lot of resources, and the more important one, time. Less than 600 pupils would also bring about problems of representativeness. Hence, 600 is considered appropriate number for the sample.

Only the **pupils studying in tenth class** in secondary schools of Guntur district, Andhra Pradesh are included in the sample. This decision is taken because the children's attitudes and aptitudes get formed intensively at the age of 14 or 15. The biology of tenth class decides their career at +2 stage.

A **sample of 600 tenth class pupils** is taken into consideration. Out of the total sample, 300 pupils are from rural schools and 300 pupils are from urban schools. All the pupils selected from rural schools are of Telugu medium as there are no English medium school in rural area. Regarding the type of school, 120 pupils are from residential school and 180 are from non-residential schools. As regards to the management of schools, 210 pupils are from government schools and 90 are from private schools in rural area. An equal representation is given to both boys and girls in the rural sample. As regards the schools in urban area, 180 pupils are selected from Telugu medium schools and 120 are selected from English medium schools. Out of these 300 pupils, 90 are from government schools and 210 are from private schools. In this urban area also, equal proportion is given to both boys and girls. With the above splitting of the total sample into various strata, the final sub-group sample sizes are: boys - 300 and girls-300, rural-300 and urban-300, private schools-300 and government schools-300, Telugu medium-480 and English medium-120, and residential schools-120 and non-residential schools-480. Thus, the total sample (600) is split into different groups.

The tools occupy a major role in any research study because they are useful in the collection of data to draw the conclusions. Construction and standardization of a good tool itself is a major research work. As the present study is a deliberate and intensive one, the available standardized tools are employed. Scientific Attitude Scale of J. K. Sood and R. P. Sanadhya, and The Kerala University Science Aptitude Test of Nair, et al. are used to study scientific attitude and scientific aptitude of secondary school pupils respectively.

CONCLUSIONS AND DISCUSSIONS

Science education has become part and parcel of human life, without which we cannot live comfortably. Identifying the multifarious values of science education, it is included in the school curriculum as a compulsory subject.

Scientific attitude is necessary to an individual to lead a smooth and comfortable life in the society. An individual with good scientific attitude can understand the phenomena of nature and human behaviour, and accordingly he will behave to prove himself an ideal individual in his own family as well as in the society in which he lives.

Scientific aptitude is necessary for pupils to pursue science education. Without having sizable amount of scientific aptitude, one cannot pursue science education properly and of course even one cannot adjust in the daily life too.

The present study has resulted in drawing the following conclusions which may be utilized in improving the present state of affairs in the school science education.

Scientific Attitude

The scientific attitude in secondary school pupils is average. The distribution of this scientific attitude in the tenth class pupils is normal. Davis, Caldwell and Lundeen, Gopal Krishna and Keurst found that the pupils were superstitious. Here, our problem is why this sample holds an average level of scientific attitude and how it can be developed and promoted more than the existing level. The facilities like library, laboratory, audio-visual aids, exposure to eminent personalities, participation in fairs, exhibitions, etc., will help in the inculcation and promotion of scientific attitude in the individuals. The above mentioned facilities are not so abundantly available in our schools, particularly in government schools. Another significant feature is the possession of scientific attitude by the teachers, who teach it, has influence directly or indirectly in the classrooms. A teacher without proper scientific attitude cannot develop or promote it. The studies of Bhaskara Rao, Sundara Rao and Mohan Rao and Bhaskara Rao, et al have identified the experienced and prospective science teachers held low scientific attitude respectively. The above mentioned factors may be the reasons for the average level of scientific attitude possessed by the secondary school pupils. Now, it is the right time for the identification of the necessary factors for the promotion of scientific attitude in the school children. Some of the factors necessary for the promotion of scientific attitudes are: Informative experiences about the attitude object, situations arising in solving a problem, pleasant emotional experiences, well - equipped science labs, group decision making, encouragement in the cultivation of desirable attitude; engag ing in wide reading in general science, preservation of democratic procedures, suggesting problems that need to collect evidences to form conclusions, stressing the need for adequate data before arriving at conclusions; through assimilation of environment, through the emotional effects, through traumatic experiences, through direct intellectual processes, providing opportunity for the analysis of problem, amount of scientific knowledge or exposure to general science courses; work experience; providing proper laboratory facilities; taking the pupils to fairs, exhibitions, excursions, field trips, zoos parks, industries, natural habitants of plants and animals; through direct teaching of the required scientific attitude, allowing the pupils to mingle with various peer and intellectual groups; exposing them to the eminent personalities like scientists, social reformers, etc.

All the science educators must try to promote the scientific attitude in the pupils by implementing the above mentioned factors that are feasible in their own educational set up.

The scientific attitude in both boys and girls is average and there is no difference in the level of scientific attitude possessed by them. The distribution of scientific attitude in these two groups is also normal. As the sample is from the coeducational schools, except A.P. Residential Schools, this result states that if the opportunities are equal to either sex, they can compete with each other equally in any area. This is in contrary to the result of the study made by Shrivastava. The science teacher must try to promote scientific attitude in the pupils through the above suggested procedures.

The scientific attitude possessed by the pupils in private and government schools fall under average category. The pupils of private schools hold a little bit high scientific attitude than those of government schools. But both the sub-samples are with an average scientific attitude. The distribution of it in both of them is also not normal. It is tending towards high scientific attitude category in private schools, where as it is reverse in government schools. Many people say that the facilities available in the private schools are good. The quality of teaching will also be good as there are better facilities. Another important thing for this quality is that inferior teaching will be questioned immediately without any delay, which is no possible in the case of government schools. The teachers will teach throughout a pupils school career in private schools as the teacher works in the same school for a long time without any transfers, and as he understands the flaws and potentialities of his pupils. All these factors will play a significant rôle in promoting scientific attitude, which may be adopted in government schools also.

The scientific attitude possessed by the pupils of urban and rural schools is average. The rural pupils hold high level of scientific attitude than urban pupils, but the distribution in both the sub-samples is normal. On the contrary, earlier studies of Bhaskara rao, Sundara Rao and Mohan Rao and Gopal Krishan found that the locale did not influence the possession of scientific attitude. The result of this study is a surprising one, because the urban schools are supposed to be equipped well with all facilities, and the quality of teaching may also be good as many people say. This study indicates that if conducive facilities are provided to the rural pupils they will score as better as urban pupils.

The scientific attitude in the pupils of English and Telugu medium schools is average. The English medium pupils hold a bit high scientific attitude than the Telugu medium pupils. The distribution of scientific attitude is normal only in Telugu medium pupils, but its concentration is tending towards high level in English medium pupils. Normally, if there exists any language barrier, the pupils of Telugu medium should possess better scientific attitude than those of English medium as the former understand the subject very easily as Telugu is their mother tongue. The finding of this study supports that the better facilities available in a school facilitate the development of scientific attitude.

The scientific attitude possessed by the pupils of residential and non-residential schools is average. But, when compared, the pupils of residential schools are with very high scientific attitude than those of non-residential schools. The distribution of scientific attitude is normal in the pupils of non-residential schools. The distribution of scientific attitude is normal in the pupils of nonresidential schools, but its trend is towards high level in the pupils of residential schools. The facilities that are available in A.P. Residential School are no where available either in private schools or in other government schools. The facilities that are available, the teaching learning schedule they follow, the intelligence of the pupils of residential schools might have helped in possessing such a high scientific attitude. So, these facilities may be extended to other types of schools.

It is worthwhile to consolidate the results regarding the influence of the variables on scientific attitude. **The pupils studying in private schools, rural schools, English medium schools and residential schools hold relatively better scientific attitude than their counter parts. There is no influence of sex on scientific attitude. All the pupils of the five variables hold an average scientific attitude.** The significant influence of the above variables makes it clear that the facilities that are available and the conducive teaching learning atmosphere that is prevalent in schools are the deciding factors in cultivating and promoting the scientific attitude.

Scientific Aptitude

The scientific aptitude in the secondary school pupils is average. The distribution of it in the whole sample is also normal. In a study, Jose found that 70% of 9th class pupils were with average scientific aptitude. As scientific aptitude is a potentiality for future achievement in a scientific endeavour and as it is a complex of interacting hereditary and environmental determinants producing such potentialities or predispositions of future accomplishment, it is necessary to develop scientific aptitude among the pupils. Development of scientific aptitude is dependent on a variety of factors. The presence of certain study skills; persistence in learning and motivation; satisfaction derived from learning a subject, evaluation procedures that are followed in education; cultural background; socio-economic factors; interests; attitudes are some of the important factors that promote scientific aptitude.

The scientific aptitude in boys and girls is average and the distribution of it is also normal in both the sub-samples. The teachers must try to promote and the pupils must try to attain high scientific aptitude.

The scientific aptitude is average in the pupils of private and government schools. The pupils of private schools possess a bit high scientific aptitude than those of government schools. The distribution in the two sub-sample is not normal. The scientific aptitude concentration is towards high in private schools and vice versa in government schools. The managements of government schools should provide the facilities conducive to the promotion of scientific aptitude, and the teachers must utilize the available resources in a best possible manner to promote scientific aptitude in the pupils.

The scientific aptitude in the pupils of urban and rural school is average, but the urban pupils possess a little bit high scientific aptitude than rural pupils. The distribution of scientific aptitude in both the sample is normal. The facilities that are available are the causes to be said for this difference in the scientific aptitude possessed by the urban and rural pupils. The authorities concerned should try to promote the educational facilities in rural schools.

The scientific aptitude is average in the pupils of Telugu and English medium schools. The pupils of English medium possess a little bit high scientific aptitude than those of Telugu medium. The scientific aptitude trend is towards high scientific aptitude in English medium pupils, and its trend is towards low category in Telugu medium pupils. This result states that the language plays a role in the development of scientific aptitude. But, this result may be because of the facilities that facilitate it in the English medium schools.

The scientific aptitude is average in residential and non-residential schools. But the pupils of residential schools are superior to those of non-residential schools. The trait distribution is normal in both the cases. The educational facilities that prevail in residential schools should be provided in other types of schools.

On the whole the pupils of private schools, urban schools, English medium schools and residential schools hold a bit more scientific aptitude than their counterparts. There is no significant influence of sex on the level of the possession of scientific aptitude. All the groups belonging to the five variablès hold an average level of scientific aptitude. From the above results, it is clear that the better facilities and good teaching-learning atmosphere share a major part in the inculcation and promotion of scientific aptitude.

ASSOCIATION BETWEEN SCIENTIFIC ATTITUDE AND SCIENTIFIC APTITUDE

The association between scientific attitude and scientific aptitude is highly significant and positive. It is a good sign and if we develop scientific attitude or scientific aptitude, this in turn leads to the development of the other.

The association between scientific attitude and scientific aptitude in both boys and girls is highly significant and positive. These results state that there is no influence of sex on the association of these aspects. This study gives an indication that if the opportunities are provided equally to either sex, they can compete equally in all aspects.

The association between scientific attitude and scientific aptitude in the pupils studying in private and government schools is highly significant and positive. These results indicate that where there are better educational facilities there is better association in between the traits. So, one should try to improve the physical facilities of schools as well as teaching efficiencies.

There is a high significant and positive association between scientific attitude and scientific aptitude in the pupils of urban and rural schools. The urban pupils are supposed to be exposed to more knowledge and better facilities. This may be the reason for better association among traits in urban pupils than in rural pupils. The rural pupils may be exposed to science fairs, exhibitions, zoos, parks, industries, laboratory experiments, books, etc., for better accomplishment.

The association between scientific attitude and scientific aptitude is highly significant and positive in the pupils of Telugu and English medium. There will be a language hindrance in understanding a phenomenon in English medium pupils, whereas it is a mother tongue to the telugu medium pupils. To the English medium pupils, the school and home environments are entirely different. So, there may be equal possession of the psychological traits and achievement in biology in Telugu medium pupils.

There is significant and positive association between scientific attitude and scientific aptitude in the pupils of residential and non residential schools. As there is association among the three factors, the promotion of them must be taken into consideration.

On the whole, the psychological traits, viz., scientific attitude and scientific aptitude are average in the samples. There is highly significant and positive association between scientific attitude and scientific aptitude. The science educators must try to promote the level of scientific attitude and scientific aptitude possessed by the samples. If necessary steps are taken, our pupils will accomplish and achieve any thing in science education.

SUGGESTIONS FOR FURTHER RESEARCH

The present study brings to light a good number of new areas to be studied by the future researchers. The areas and variables which are not covered by this study may be put to test to enlighten the factors associated with the inculcation and development of scientific attitude and scientific aptitude. So, the researchers may think of the following areas to study in detail.

1. Studies on scientific attitude and scientific aptitude may be extended to the other educational levels, viz., primary and college levels at district and state levels.
2. Studies may be conducted on scientific attitude and scientific aptitude either independently or combindly at various levels of education, areas and variables.
3. Studies may be taken up to find out the effect of independent variables on dependent variables in the cases of controlled and experimental groups as this study has not used any special controlled variables.

4. Studies may be conducted to find out the effect of environmental and psychological factors on the inculcation and development of scientific attitude and scientific aptitude.
5. Studied about the scientific attitude and scientific aptitude possessed by the teaching community may be taken up as this factor has a great role to play in the development of scientific attitude and scientific aptitude in the class rooms.
6. Studies can be taken up to identify the reasons for the possession of average scientific attitude and scientific aptitude as found in this study.
7. Studies may be conducted on the use of audio-visual teaching aids, laboratory and library facilities in the schools as these have greater influence on attitude and aptitude.

Bibliography

Aggarwal, K.K. *Manual for Scientific aptitude Test Battery*. Agra: National Psychological Corporation,. 1986.

Alpern, Moris L, "The Ability to Test Hypotheses". *Science Education* 30 (October 1946), 220-229.

Anderson, L.W., "Attitudes and their Measurement". *The International Encyclopedia of Educational Research and Studies* (1985), 1: 352–358

Approach Paper on Science & Mathematics in General Education, Report of the working group on Science & Mathematics, September 1985. Department of Education in Science & Mathematics, National Council of Education Research and Training, New Delhi.

Atkinson, J. Myron and R. Will Burnell, "Science Education". *Enclyclopedia of Educational Research*, 4th ed., 1192-1205.

Baumel, Howard B. and J. Joel Berger. "An attempt to Measure *Scientific Attitudes*". Science Education 49 (April 1965), 267-269.

Best John W. *Research in Education*, 4th ed. New Delhi : Prentice Hall of India Pvt. Ltd., 1982.

Bhandula, N., P. C. Chadha, S. Sharma and M.P. Bhasin. *Teaching of Science*, Ludhiana: Prakash Brothers, 1985.

Bhaskara Rao, D. *An Evaluative Study of the New Science curriculum at Upper Primary Level in Andhra Pradesh.* Unpublished Master of Education Dissertation, Nagarjuna University, Nagarjunanager, 1982.

Bhaskara Rao, D., "Effective Communication in Teaching". *Experiments in Education* XIII (August 1985), 109-111.

Bhaskara Rao, D., Objectives of Science". *Science Promoter* 2 October 1989), 701-703.

Bhaskara Rao, D., "Teacher : The Supreme of Mankind". *Education* 63 (July 1983), 193-196.

Bhaskara Rao, D., "Utilisation of Community Resources in Science Teaching". *Junior Scientist* 23 (February 1986), 5-6.

Bhaskara Rao, Digumarti, "An Evaluative Study of the New Science Curriculum at Upper Primary Level in Andhra Pradesh". *Experiments in Education* X (October 1982), 147-149.

Bhaskara Rao, Digumarti, "An Evaluative Study of the Teaching Efficiency of Prospective Biological Science Teachers", *School Science* XXVI (September 1988), 17-20.

Bhaskara Rao, Digumarti., *Audio Visual Teaching Aids.* Guntur: Nagarjuna Publishers, 1989.

Bhaskara Rao, Digumarti, "Education for Individual Responsibility". *Educational India* 48 (June 1982), 185-187.

Bhaskara Rao, Digumarti, "Effective Communication in Teaching". *Experiments in Education* XIII (April 1985), 109-111.

Bhaskara Rao, Digumarti, "Private Educational Institutions". *The Educational Review* XC (February 1984), 34-36.

Bhaskara Rao, Digumarti, "Science Education in Secondary Schools: A Reflection". *National Conference on New Education Policy; Its Need & Concept*, 10-12 October, 1987. Report and Abstract of Papers. Department of Education, Hindu college, Moradabad, 1987, 5.

Bhaskara Rao, Digumarti, "When does the state of Science Education change in Schools?". *Telugu Vidhyarthi* 36 (July 1989), 47-50.

Bhaskara Rao, D. (1994). *Scientific Aptitude.* New Delhi: Ashish publishing House.

Bhaskara Rao, D. (1994). *Teaching of Science*. Guntur: Nagarjuna Publishers

Bhaskara Rao, D. (1995). *Teaching of Biology*. Guntur: Creative Press

Bhaskara Rao, D. (1995). *Educational Psychology*. Guntur: Creative Press

Bhaskara Rao, D. (1995). *Scientific Attitude*. Ambala Cantt: The Associated Publishers.

Bhaskara Rao, D. and D. Pushpa Latha (1994). *Achievement in Biology*. New Delhi: Discovery Publishing House.

Bhaskara Rao, D. and D. Pushpa Latha (1995). *Achievement in English*. New Delhi: Discovery Publishing House.

Bhaskara Rao, D. and D. Pushpa Latha (1995). *Achievement in Mathematics*. New Delhi: Discovery Publishing House.

Bhaskara Rao, D. and D. Pushpa Latha (1995). *Achievement in Science*. New : Discovery Publishing House.

Bhaskara Rao, D., K. Vijaya and C. Sridevi (1995). *Achievement in Social Studies*. New Delhi: Discovery Publishing House.

Bhaskara Rao, D. and K. Vijaya (1995). *A Textbook Evaluation*. Ambala Cantt: The Indian Publishers.

Bhaskara Rao, D., D. Eliah and G. Sundara Rao, "Pedagogic Aptitude of In-service and pre-service Teachers". *The Educational Review* XCIII (April 1987), 61-64.

Bhaskara Rao, D., G. Sunmdra Rao and S. Raja Mohan Rao., "Scientific Attitudes of Experienced Science Teachers at Secondary School level". *The Educational Review* XCII (April 1986), 60-65.

Bhaskara Rao, D., G. Sundara Rao and S. Aruna and L. Rathaiah, "Scientific Attitudes and Personality Traits of Prospective Science Teachers". *Progressive Educational Herald* 3 (January 1989), 62-66.

Bhaskara Rao, Digumarti and Vijaya Lakshmi, D., "An Evaluative Study of the New Science syllabus of class VII in A.P." *Educational India* 49 (August 1982), 19-22.

Bhaskara Rao, D., G. Sundara Rao and D.V.D. Malleswari, "Teachers Opinions towards the Appeal of Pictorial Representation and Motivational Quality of suggested Activities in Science Text Books at Primary Level in Andhra Pradesh". *Educational India* 53 (January 1987), 102-104.

Bhaskara Rao, D., G. Sundara Rao and L., Rathaiah, "The Science teacher has a definite role". *The Hindu* (September 27,1988), 19.

Bhaskara Rao, D., G. Sundara Rao and V. Bhaskara Reddy, "Conceptulisation Facility in General Science Text Book of Class VII in Andhra Pradesh." *Educational India* 53 (December 1986), 87-90.

Bhaskara Rao, D., G. Yashoda, D. Eliah and G. Sundara Rao, "Individual Modernity of In-service and Pre-service Teachers". *Experiments in Education* XIV (September 1986), 127-129.

Bhaskara Rao, D., L. Rathaiah, G. Sundara Rao and M. Vijaya Lakshmi, "Attitude of Urban Graduate Science Teachers towards the use of Visual Aids in class Room Teaching." *The Educational Review* XCII (August 1987), 133-135.

Bhaskara Rao, D., S. Aruna and G. Sundara Rao, "Scientific Attitudes and Personality Traits of Prospective Science Teachers". *Journal of the Institute of Educational Research* 11 (May 1987), 1-4.

Biswas, A. and J.C. Aggarwal. *Encyclopaedic Dictionary and Directory of Education*, Vol. 1. New Delhi: The Academic Publishers (India), 1987.

Brunkhorst, Herbert K. and Robert E. Yager, "A New Rationale for Science Education". *The Education Digest* (December 1986), 24-27.

Burmester, Mary Alice. "The construction and validation of a Test to measure some of the Inductive Aspects of Scientific Thinking". *Science Education* 37 (March 1953), 131-140.

Bloom, Benjamin S., ed., *Taxonomy of Educational Objectives, Hand Book 1: Cognitive Domain*. New York: Longman, Green and co., 1959.

Brandwein, Paul F., Fletcher G. Watson and Paul E. Blackwood. *A Book of Methods*. New York: Harcourt, Brace & World, Inc., 1958.

Buch, M.B., ed., *Second Survey of Research in Education*, Baroda : Society for Educational Research and Development, 1979.

Buch, M. B., Chief Editor. *Third Survey of Research in Education*. New Delhi: National Council of Educational Research and Training. 1987.

Burnett, R. Will. *Teaching Science in the Secondary Schools.* New York: Holt, Rinehart and Winston, 1960.

Caldwell, Otis W. and Francis D. Curtis. *Everyday Science.* Boston: Ginn and Co., 1943.

Caldwell, O. W. and Gerhard E. Lundeen, "Students' Attitudes regarding unfounded Beliefs". *Science Education* 15 (May 1931), 246-266.

Chhikara, M.S. and S. Sharma. *Teaching of Biology.* Ludhiana: Prakash Brothers, 1985.

Das, R. C. *Science Teaching in Schools.* New Delhi; Sterling Publishers Pvt. Ltd., 1985.

Davis, Ira C. "The Measurement of Scientific Attitudes". *Science Education* 19 (October 1935), 117-122.

Desai, D. B. and Ameeta Govind. *Studies in Achievement Motivation.* Baroda: Centre for Advanced Study in Education, M.S. University of Baroda, 1979.

Diederich, Paul B., "Components of the Scientific Attitude". *The Science Teacher* 34 (February 1967), 23-24.

Downing, Elliot R., "Some Results of a Test on Scientific Thinking". *Science Education* 20 (October 1936), 121.

Ebel, Robert L, "What is the Scientific Attitude/". *Science Education* 22 (January 1938), 1-5.

Ebel, Robert L., "What is the scientific Attitude?". *Science Education* 22 (February 1938), 75-81.

English, H. B. and A. C. English. *A Comprehensive Dictionary of Psychoanalytical Terms.* London: Longmans, 1958.

Restinger, Leon and Katz Daniel. *Research Methods in the Behavioural Sciences.* Amerind Publishing co., 1976.

Freeman, Frank s. *Theory and Practice of Psychological* Testing, 3rd ed. Calcutta: Oxford & IBH Publishing Co., 1965.

Gage, N.L., *Handbook of Research on Teaching.* Chicago: Rand McNally & Co., 1966.

Garret, Henry E. *Statistics in Psychology and Education.* Bombay: Peffer and Simons Pvt. Ltd., 1979.

Gauld, Colin, "The Scientific Attitude and Science Education: A Critical Reappraisal". *Science Education* 66 (1982), 109-121.

Gauld, C.F. and A.A. Haukins. "Scientific Attitudes: A Review". *Studies in Science Education* 7 (1980), 129-161.

General Science Sub-committee of the Science masters" Association. *Report on the Teaching of General Science*. London: John Murray, 1960.

Good, C.V., ed. *Dictionary of Education*. New York: McGraw Hill Book co., 1959.

Goode, William J. and Paul K. Hatt. *Methods in Social Research*. Tokyo: McGraw Hill International Book Co., 1983.

Green, T.L., *The Teaching of Biology in Tropical Secondary Schools*. Vol. X of the UNESCO Handbooks on the Teaching of Science in Tropical countries. London: Oxford University press, 1965.

Gupta, Arun Kumar, "Differential Scientific Aptitude Abilities and Scholastic Achievement". *Indian Educational Review* XX (October 19850, 151-157.

Haney, Richard E., "The Development of Scientific Attitude". *The Science Teacher* 31 (December 1984). 33-35.

Henry, Nelson B., ed. *Rethinking Science Education*. The fifty ninth yearbook of the National Society for the Study of Education, Part-1, 1960. Distributed by the University of Chicago Press, Chicago, Illinois, 1960.

Heiss, Eldwood D., Ellsworth S. Obourn and Charles W. Hoffman. *Modern Science Teaching*. New York: The Macmillan Co., 1950.

Hurd, P. H., "The Educational Concepts of the Secondary Science Teaching". *School Science and Mathematics* (1954), 89-96.

Hutchings, Donal, ed. *Towards More Creative Science*. New College Conference, June 1966. Oxford: Pergamon Press, 1966.

Jacobson, Willard J. and Rodney L. Doran. *Science Achievement in the United States and Sixteen Countries*. The International Association for the Evaluation of Educational Research, Second IEA Science Study. Teachers College, Columbia University, new York, 1988.

Jenkins, E. W., "Science Education, History of ", *The International Encylcopedia of Education Research and Studies*. (1985) 8: 4453-4456.

Jayaswal, Sita Ram. *Techniques and Tests in Psychology and Education.* Lucknow: Prakashan Kendra, 1968.

Kalra, R.M. *Innovations in Science Teaching.* New Delhi: Oxford & IBH Publishing co., 1976.

Keil, L., J., "Attitude Development". *The International Encyclopedia of Education Research and Studies,* (1985) 1: 346-352.

Kennedy, P.J. and A. Loria. *Proceedings of the International Conference on Education for Physics Teaching.* TRIESTE, Ist-6th September 1980. The International Commission on Physics Education, Physics Department, University of Edinburgh, Edinburgh, Scotland, 1980.

Kerlinger, Fred N. *Foundations of Behavioural Research.* Holt, Rinehart & Winston, 1964.

Keurst, Arthur J. Ker, "The Acceptance of Superstitious Beliefs among Secondary School Pupils". *Journal of Educational Research* 32 (May 1939), 673-685.

K.M., Jose. *A Comparative Study of the Biology Achievement of High. Average: And Low-Science aptitude of Secondary School Pupils.* Unpublished Master of Education Thesis, University of Calicut, Calicut, 1987.

Krishan, D. Gopal. *A Study of Scientific Attitude and its Relation to Intelligence of Graduate Students.* Unpublished Master of Education Dissertation, Andhra University, Waltair, 1975.

Kozlow, James M. and Marshall A. Nay, "An Approach to Measure Scientific Attitudes". *Science Education* 60 (April-June 1976), 147-172.

Lampkin Jr., Richard H., "Scientific Attitudes". *Science Education* 22 (December 1938), 353-357.

Libert, Robert M. and John M. Neale. *Psychology.* New York: John Wiley & Sons, Inc., 1977.

Lonk, F., "An Approach to a more Adequate systems of Evaluation in Science " *The Science Teacher* 34 (1967), 20-24.

Maybury, Robert H. and Adolph Y. Wilbrun, "science Education, International". *The Encyclopedia of Education* 8: 107-117.

Miller, David F. and Clenn W. Blaydes. *Methods and Materials for Teaching the Biological Sciences.* Bombay: Tata McGraw Hill Publishing Pvt. Ltd., 1962.

Ministry of Education, Government of India, *Challenge of Education-A Policy Perspective*, 1985.

Ministry of Human Resource Development, Department of Education, Government of India. *National Policy on Education*-1986.

Murty, K. Satchidananda. *New Education Policy: Some Reflections and Reactions.* Principal Address, State level Seminar on New Education Policy, T.J.P.S. College, Guntur, 1985.

Nair, A.S. and S. Joseph. *An Experimental Study of the overlap of Intelligence and Science attitude with Educational outcomes in Biology measured using Host's Taxonomy.* Department of Education, University of Kerala, Trivandrum, 1978.

National Scheme of Inservice Training for School Teachers. *Resource Material Part I, General.* New Delhi: National Council of Educational Research and Training, 1987.

National Scheme of Inservice Training for School Teachers. *Resource Material, Part II Secondary.* New Delhi : National Council of Educational Research and Training. 1987.

Noll, Victor H., "Measuring the Scientific Attitude". *Journal of Abnormal and Social Psychology* 30 (July 1935), 145-146.

Okey, James R., "The Scientific Attitude and Science Education : A Critical Reappraisal". *Science Education* 66 (1982), 109-121.

Patnaik , Nalini Prabha., "Achievement in General Science of Class V children of Berhampur, Orissa- A Research Study". *School Science* XXIV (March 1986), 47-50.

Pearl, Richard E., "The Present Status of Science Attitude Measurement: History, Theory, and Availability of Measurement Instruments". *School Science and Mathematics* LXXIV (May-June 1974), 375-381.

Peterson, Rita W. and Gaylon R. Carlson. "A summary of Research in *Science Education*-1977". Science Education 63 (1979).

Pillai, Kamala S., "The Relative Efficiency of Science Aptitude and Intelligence to Predict Biology Achievement". *Experiments in Education* XIV (December 1986), 171-175.

Programme of Mass Orientation for School Teachers. *Inservice Teacher Education Package, Vol I: For Primary School Teachers.* New Delhi: National Council of Educational Research and Training, 1988.

Programme of Mass Orientation for School Teachers. *Inservice Teacher Education Vol. II: For Upper Primary & Secondary School Teachers.* New Delhi: National Council of Educational Research and Training, 1988.

Rai, B. C. *Methods of Teaching Science.* Lucknow: Prakashan Kendra, 1983.

Rathaiah, L. And D. Bhaskara Rao (1995). *Achievement Correlates.* Ambala Cantt: The Indian Publications.

Ravindranath, M. J., "Development of Scientific Attitude: An Experimental Study". *Journal of India Education* (November 1983), 28-32.

Reader's Digest. *Great Illustrated Dictionary, A-K,* London: The Readers Digest Association Ltd., 1984.

Reif, Frederick., "Scientific Approaches to Science Education". *Physics Today* (November 1986), 38-44.

Richardson, John S., Stanely E. Williamson and Donald W. Stotler. *The Education Science Teachers.* Columbus, Ohio: Charles E. Merril Publishing company, 1968.

Rummel, J. Francis. *An Introduction to Research Procedures in Education.* New York: Harper and Brothers, 1958.

Saunders, H.N. *The Teaching of General Science in Tropical Secondary Schools.* Vol. VII of the UNESCO handbooks on the Teaching of Science in Tropical countries. London: Oxford University Press, 1959.

Saxena, K.N., "A comparative Study of the Achievement in Science of Urban and rural Students". *Journal of Education and Psychology* 21 (1963), 38-44.

Schibeci, R.A., "Selecting Appropriate Attitudinal Objectives for School Science". *Science Education* 67 (October 1983), 595-603.

Science Education in Asia and the Pacific, Bulletin of the UNESCO Regional Office for Education in Asia and the Pacific, Number 25, Bangkok: UNESCO Regional Office for Education in Asia and the pacific, 1984.

Secondary Modern Schools Sub-committee of the Science Masters' Association. *Secondary Modern Science Teaching,* Part I. London: John Murray, 1964.

Sharma, R.C. *Modern Science Teaching.* Delhi: Dhanpat Rai & Sons, 1984.

Shrivastava. N.N., "A Study of the Scientific Attitude and its Measurement". *Indian Educational Review* (January 1983), 95-97.

Shukla, U. C. *Kothari Commission Report.* Lucknow: Prakashan Kendra, 1977.

Siddiqi, N.N. And M.N. Siddiqi. *Teaching of Science Today and Tomorrow.* Delhi: Doaba House, 1983.

Sing Pritam. *A Monograph on Improving Practical Examinations in Science.* New Delhi: National Council of Educational Research and Training. 1983.

Singh , Raja Ray. *Education in Asia and the Pacific—Retrospect: Prospect.* Bangkok: UNESCO Regional office for Education in Asia and the Pacific, 1986.

Skaria, S. *A Study of the Attainment of Essential concepts in Biology in Relation to Science Aptitude of Secondary School Pupils.* Unpublished master of Education Thesis, University of Calicut, Calicut, 1984.

State Council of Educational Research and Training. *Year Plans- Model Lesson Plans, Biology, 9th Class.* Hyderabad: S.C.E.R.T., 1976.

Smith, Edward W., Stanely W. Krouse. Jr. and Mark M. Atkinson. *The Educator's Encyclopedia.* Englewood Cliffs, new Jercy: Prentice Hall, Inc., 1967.

Sumangala, V., "Effect of Attitude towards mathematics and Sex on Achievement in Mathematics. *Experiments in Education* XVI (July 1988). 156-161.

Sood, J.K., ed. *Emerging Perspectives in Science Education Research.* Ajmer: Regional college of Education, 1978.

Sood, J.K. *New Directions in Science Teaching.* Chandigarh: Kohli Publishers, 1989.

Sood, J.K. *Teaching Life Sciences- A Book of Methods.* Chandigarh: Kohli Publisher, 1987.

Sreekumar, S. *A Comparative Study of Science Interest, Science Aptitude and Science Achievement in Science club members and non-members of High School.* Unpublished Master of Education Dissertation, University of Kerala, Trivandrum, 1972.

Sujatha, Kumari B. *The Relative Effeciency of Science Aptitude, Science Interest and Attitude towards Science in Predicting Biology Achievement of Secondary School Pupils.* Unpublished master of Education Thesis, University of Calicut, Calicut, 1987.

Sundararajan, S., "Higher Secondary Students' Achievement in Biology". *Experiments in Education* XVII (March 1989), 58-66.

Sukhia, S. P., P. V. Mehrotra and R. N. Mehrotra. *Elements of Educational Research.* New Delhi: Allied Publishers Pvt. Ltd., 1980

Thampy, M.P. *A Study of the Interaction of Science Aptitude and Attitude towards Science on Biology Achievement of Secondary School Pupils.* Unpublished Master of Education Thesis, University of Calicut, Calicut, 1984.

The New Encyclopedia Britanica, Macropaedia, Vol. 2. 15th ed. Chicago: Encyclopedia Britanica, Inc., 1984.

The Readers Digest. *Great Encyclopaedic Dictionary.* Vol. I, A-L. London: The Reader's Digest Association, 1962.

Thurber, Walter A. and Alfred T. Collette. *Teaching Science in Today's Secondary Schools* 3rd ed. Boston: Allyn and Bacon, Inc., 1968.

UNESCO. *Learning to be.* New Delhi: National Council of Educational Research and Training, 1974.

Vaidya, Narendra. *Problem Solving in Science.* Delhi: S. Chand & Co., 1967.

Vaidya, Narendra. *The Impact Science Teaching.* New Delhi: Oxford & IBH Publishing Co., 1976.

Vaidya, Narendra and J.S. Rajput, eds. *Reshapping our School Science Education.* New Delhi: Oxford and IBH Publishing co., 1977.

Venkata Rao, P. and D. Bhaskara Rao. *A Test Book of Zoology- Junior Intermediate.* revised Edition. Guntur: Vigyan Publishers, 1989.

Venkata Rao, P. and D. Bhaskara Rao. *A Test Book of zoology- Senior Intermediate.* Revised Edition. Guntur: Vigyan publishers, 1989.

Vessel, M. F. *Elementary School Science Teaching.* New Delhi: Prentice Hall of India (Pvt) Ltd., 1965.

Victor, Edward and Marjorie S. Lernar. *Readings in Science Education for the Elementary School.* New York: The Macmilan co., 1967.

Wanchoo, V.N., ed. *World Views on Science Education*. Oxford & IBH Publishing co., 1982.

Wanchoo, V.N. and T.N. Raina, eds. *Research in Science & Mathematics Education*. Ajmer: Regional college of Education, 1976.

Warters, Jane. *Techniques of Counselling*. New York: MacGraw Hill, 1954.

Washton, Nathan S. *Science Teaching in the Secondary Schools*. New York: Harper & Brothers, 1961.

Williams, S.S., "A Comparative Study of the Achievement of Rural and urban Secondary Pupils in General Science". *Journal of the Institute of Educational Research* 3 (1979), 33-34.

Williams, Sarah S., "A comparative Study of Pupils' Achievement in some of the Instructional Objectives in Teaching General Science". *Experiments in Education* XV (1987), 67-73.

Witting, Arnof. *Theory and Problems of Introduction to Psychology*. New York: McGraw Hill Book co., 1977.

Wrightstone, J.W., et al. *Education in Modern Education*. New York; American Book co., 1956.

Young, Pauline V. and Calvin F. Schmid. *Scientific Social Surveys and Research*. New Delhi: Prentice Hall of India Pvt. Ltd., 1968.

Appendices

APPENDIX–A

SCIENTIFIC ATTITUDE SCALE

Instructions

The following statements are concerned with Scientific Attitude. Read each statement carefully and then mark your answer on the sheet. Work rapidly. Record your first impression, the feeling that comes to your mind, as you read the item.

Draw a circle around **SA** if you strongly or fully agree with an item. Draw a circle around **A** if you are in partial agreement with the item. Draw a circle around **N** if you are neutral. Draw a circle around **D** if you partially disagree. Draw a circle around **SD** if you strongly or totally disagree. Answer all statements.

1. Now it is not possible to develop more sensitive x-ray machine. SA A N D SD
2. To challenge the Bible that 'the sun revolves round the earth' was not the right step of Copernicus. SA A N D SD
3. A conclusion based on insufficient evidences should neither be accepted nor be rejected. SA A N D SD
4. An idea should not be accepted if it is proved to be poor. SA A N D SD

5. The scientists should have to find out the occurrences of the undesired events in nature. SA A N D SD
6. The ideas are true if few facts support them. SA A N D SD
7. Scientists should be curious to find out the occurrences of the undesired events in nature. SA A N D SD
8. Every novel situation should not be viewed in an interrogate war. SA A N D SD
9. After observing the astonishing situations like magic, a person should not strive to know the secret of it. SA A N D SD
10. Until they achieve success, the scientists should continue their efforts in collecting complete information about the Mars. SA A N D SD
11. Scientists shall be able to forecast the sex of a foetus in future. SA A N D SD
12. Science students should be eager to conduct new experiments. SA A N D SD
13. A senior scientist should not accept the new techniques suggested by another. SA A N D SD
14. One scientist should not give the right to another scientist to defy his established law. SA A N D SD
15. Positive criticism benefits the advancements of knowledge. SA A N D SD
16. The scientist B should modify his erroneous concepts if scientist A presents the correct and fully tested facts before him. SA A N D SD
17. In perspective of new discoveries and inventions, a scientist should be ready to change his prevalent conceptions. SA A N D SD

18. People should be willing to change the ideas if sufficient evidences about the hollowness of their ideas are available. SA A N D SD
19. It is impossible to defy widely held assumption in society since very long time. SA A N D SD
20. We should not believe that smallpox, cholera and other diseases are the products of devine anger. SA A N D SD
21. If one sneezes at the time of commencing a new task, one should start it later. SA A N D SD
22. Cooked stories by astrologers and magicians should not be preferred to scientifically based explanations. SA A N D SD
23. For weather predictions, magicians and astrologers should not be consulted. SA A N D SD
24. A scientist should not start his work when the way is crossed by a cat. SA A N D SD
25. At the time of drawing inferences the scientist should draw only those conclusions which coincide with the present political ideologies. SA A N D SD
26. Unacceptable new idea by all people should not be given due consideration. SA A N D SD
27. Enough evidence supporting a certain idea should be provided before that idea is accepted. SA A N D SD
28. People should read only those news papers which are in consonance with their political ideologies. SA A N D SD
29. The scientist should draw inferences on the basis of accurate observation. SA A N D SD
30. If a tea company offers a bribe to any scientist, then he should not disclose the research finding about the adverse effects of tea. SA A N D SD

31. Knowledge once accepted should not be put to test. SA A N D SD
32. When traditional beliefs are in conflict with scientific discoveries, it is better to accept the traditional beliefs. SA A N D SD
33. Due to fast explosion of knowledge, facts and theories which stand true today may be disproved tommorrow. SA A N D SD
34. Although a new theory propounded by a senior and experienced "scientist A" raised some doubts in the mind of a junior and young "scientist B". Then "scientist B" should accept "scientist A's" theory. SA A N D SD
35. More importance should be given to the traditional beliefs than the new discoveries of science. SA A N D SD
36. If a science teacher fails to arrive at the expected results during demonstration, he should try to discuss the possible cause of his failure. SA A N D SD

APPENDIX–B

KERALA UNIVERSITY SCIENCE APTITUDE TEST

INSTRUCTIONS

In this test booklet, there are five different types of tests. Instructions regarding each type of test are given in the appropriate places. You are requested to complete each type of test within the stipulated time. Answer sheet is supplied to you separately wherein there are spaces for answering each test.

In the answer sheet you have to mark **+ mark** in the appropriate places. Please take special care not to mark or write any thing in this question paper booklet. Answer each carefully and quickly as far as possible. In case you make a **+ mark** in a wrong place and if you want to mark at right place, then you black the wrong place and make a **+ mark** again in the correct place.

TURN THE PAGE ONLY WHEN YOU ARE ASKED TO DO SO

TEST–1 : NUMBER SERIES

Instructions

Numbers are arranged in a particular sequence in the following lines. In each line one or more numbers are omitted. Such places are shown with "-----------" (blanks). Moreover, the last blank in each line is shown separately.

Read the numbers in each line and understand the sequence and find out the number to be placed in the place of X. On the right side against the line answers are given under A, B, C, D, E groups. From these choices find out the correct answer and make a + mark in the appropriate circle.

Note : You need only to find out the numbers that are in the X place only.

Example	Choices A	B	C	D	E	Answer Sheet A	B	C	D	E
1. 2 3 4 5 6 ------ 8 X	6	7	8	9	10	O	O	O	O	⊕
2. 16 14 12 10 ------ 64 X	8	5	3	1	2	⊕	O	O	O	O

START when you are asked to do so. Time 15 minutes.

									CHOICES A	B	C	D	E
1.	3	6	12	24	--	96	X		192	152	162	132	102
2.	64	32	16	--	4	x			1	10	3	12	2
3.	6	7	14	15	30	31	x		60	59	61	62	63
4.	53	50	48	45	43	--	38	X	31	35	33	37	32
5.	6	8	12	20	36	X			60	64	68	54	50
6.	23	26	29	33	37	42	X		45	44	47	48	46
7.	96	90	84	--	72	--	X		60	64	58	56	62

8. 14 19 17 22 20 25 -- X 28 27 20 26 24

9. 2 4 6 12 15 30 34 X 38 64 68 54 48

10. 82 80 76 70 -- 52 X 60 45 50 55 40

11. 37 30 24 10 15 -- X 6 7 8 9 10

12. 18 19 21 22 24 25 -- X 29 26 27 28 30

13. 2 4 6 12 14 28 X 56 52 48 32 30

14. 3 4 6 9 13 -- X 18 22 24 27 15

15. 23 30 24 30 25 -- X 20 27 21 25 23

16. 6 7 8 7 8 8 89 X 8 9 10 11 12

17. 5 6 14 -- 30 X 35 39 40 41 45

18. 40 35 30 26 22 19 X 15 16 17 14 13

19. 161 81 41 21 11 X 6 3 1 2 3

20. 11 14 17 21 25 30 -- X 41 40 39 38 37

21. 42 45 15 18 6 9 -- X 6 7 5 4 3

22. 31 30 15 14 7 6 -- X 5 4 3 2 1

23. 5 6 4 12 13 11 33 X 34 31 66 32 35

24. 1 4 9 -- 25 36 -- X 64 56 81 78 61

TURN THE PAGE ONLY WHEN YOU ARE ASKED TO DO SO

TEST–2 : SCIENCE INFORMATION

Instructions

Read the following each statement and decide whether they are right or wrong. If it is right make a + mark in the circle below T (True) in the answer sheet—indicating the number of the statements. If it is wrong make + mark in the circle below F (False).

Example	Answer Sheet	
A. Iron is a metal	⊕	O
B. Magnet does not attract iron.	O	⊕

START when you are asked to do so. Time 5 minutes.

1. The radios in our houses can produce themselves songs and speech.
2. Nylon and terlin clothes are not make of natural fibres like cotton clothes.
3. Man has sent artificical satellite far beyond the stars.
4. In comparison with rough floor we can walk quickly on smooth floor.
5. We cannot see electricity.
6. It is not possible to find out the direction of arrival of a jet plane by listening to the direction of the sound it produces.
7. The primary purpose of keeping water plants in an aquarium is for its fish to get sufficient oxygen.
8. It will take more time to be benefitted by the plants if we apply artificial manure to the plants.
9. The basic components of ice and water are one and of the same.
10. It is possible to cultivate rose flowers of different colours in one rose plant.
11. One kilometer distance is longer than one mile distance.
12. If we fill an empty vessel with a little gas and cover the vessel tightly, the gas will not occupy the whole space inside the vessel.
13. An egg that is at the bottom of a glass of water will rise up if powdered salt is put into the glass.

14. The rabbit and the rat do not have the same food habit.
15. When there is sunlight, plants convert the atmospheric oxygen into CO_2.
16. In the ordinary temperature all the metals are not seen in the solid form.
17 Since it has the capacity to withstand heat opuntia grows even in the desert.
18. If we cut away the leaves of a banana plant which has fruits, the growth of the fruits will be affected.
19. The ice piece that is floating on a full glass of water, when melts and becomes water, will over flow.
20. Rainbow is seen only on rainy days.

TEST – 3 : FORMULATION

Instructions

In this test there are 10 simple arithmetic problems. Work out the problem mentally. Under each question there are five answers. Find out the correct one and make a + mark in the appropriate place in the answer sheet.

Example | **Answer Sheet**

	A	B	C	D	E
1. If 5X = 10, what is the value of X ? (A) 10 (B) 5 (C) 2 (D) 15 (E) 3	O	O	⊕	O	O
2. If X and Y are two numbers, what is the total ? (A) X+Y (B) XY (C) X–Y (D) Y (E) 2XY	⊕	O	O	O	O

START when you are asked to do so. Time 8 mts.

1. The hour hand of a clock turns X° in each hour. How many degrees it will turn in 'h' hours ?

   (A) $\frac{60X}{h}$ (B) 60 Xh (C) $\frac{Xh}{60}$ (D) Xh (E) $\frac{Xh}{12}$

2. If X shows one side of a square, how will you show its area ?

   (A) 2X (B) X^2 (C) X+4 (D) 4X (E) $\sqrt{X}$

3. How many hours a 60 watt bulb burns by using the current required for burning a bulb of 100 watt for X hours ?

   (A) $\frac{100}{60X}$ (B) $\frac{60}{100X}$ (C) $\frac{60X}{100}$ (D) $\frac{100X}{60}$ (E) $\frac{60}{X}$

4. The strength required (F) to break a big rope can be calculated by taking the rope's perimeter (c)'s square and multiplying it with a fixed number (e). Make a formula.

   (A) F=ec (B) $F=\frac{e}{c}$ (C) $F=e^2c$ (D) $F=c^2e$ (E) $F=e^2c^2$

5. Out of two pieces of iron, the bigger one weighs 4 pounds less than the double of the smaller one. If the smaller one weighs X pounds, what is the weight of the bigger one ?

   (A) X–4 (B) $\frac{X-4}{2}$ (C) $\frac{X}{2}+4$ (D) 2X–4 (E) (X–4) 2

6. If an aeroplane travels 'm' kilometers in 'h' hours and 'n' kms. in 'k' hours, what is the average speed of the aeroplane ?

(A) $\frac{h=k}{m+n}$ (B) $\frac{hk}{mn}$ (C) $\frac{h}{2m}+\frac{k}{2n}$

(D) $\frac{m}{2h}+\frac{h}{2k}$ (E) $\frac{m+n}{h+k}$

7. In a measuring jar there is Xcc of water. If we put 'n' number of iron balls each having 2cc volume, what will be the reading of the water surface in the measuring jar ?

(A) 2nx (B) x+2n (C) 2n–x (D) (x–n) (E) 2x+n

8. The pressure exerted by the water in a vessel at its bottom is proportionate to the depth of water. When the depth is 'd' the pressure is 'k' when the depth is 'r' and the pressure is 'z'. If so find out the relationship of the four ?

(A) d+r = Z+k (B) $\frac{d}{r}=\frac{z}{k}$ (C) $\frac{d}{r}-\frac{k}{2}$

(D) k = dkr (E) dr = kz

9. For a rectangle the length is double the breadth. If the breadth is 'w' what is the perimeter of the rectangle ?

(A) 4w+2 (B) 2w (C) 6w (D) 8w (E) 4w

10. A spring elongated 'a' cm when 'f' force is applied. Find out the formula for the force required (F) to elongate it 'b' cms.

(A) $F=\frac{f}{ab}$ (B) $F=\frac{fb}{a}$ (C) F=fab

(D) $F=\frac{af}{b}$ (E) $F=\frac{ab}{£}$

TURN THE PAGE ONLY WHEN YOU ARE ASKED TO DO SO

TEST–4 : SPATIAL ABILITY

Instructions

Each test item consists of a picture. Six answers are given for each item. You have to find out which pictures are the correct ones, when the first one is rotated to the right or left side, and you have to mark the response in the answer sheet. There may be 2 or 3 correct answers for each item.

Example

Scoring Key

A	B	C	D	E	F
O	O	⊕	O	⊕	⊕
⊕	O	O	O	⊕	O

START when you are asked to do so. Time 18 mts.

A B C D E F

TURN THE PAGE ONLY WHEN YOU ARE ASKED TO DO SO

TEST – 5 : VERBAL COMPREHENSION AND INTERPRETATION

Instructions

Some paragraphs are given below under 4 sections. Under each section, the related questions and incomplete statements with answers are given. Read the paragraph and find out the correct answer and correct words to complete the statements, put a + marke in the appropriate circles in the answer sheet.

START when you are asked to do so. TIME 13 mts.

Digestion takes place to a great extent in the stomach. The gastric juice that is secreted by the cells of the stomach wall contains an enzyme called pepsin and hydrochloric acid. pH level conducive for the digestion of protein is supplied to pepsin by hydrochloric acid.

Here arises an interesting problem. Though the gastric juice is a powerful liquid which as the ability to digest protein, why doesn't it digest the stomach wall which is made up of (mainly) protein. So far much is not known about it. However, certain cells in the stomach wall produce a mucous substance and this substance covers the whole stomach wall and protects the cells of the stomach wall. Experiencing strong emotions like fear and anger at the time of taking food will prevent the production of mucous substance. Unfortunately, when the self-protecting devices of the stomach fail to function, the stomach wall also occasionally undergoes digestion and the ulcers result.

1. pH required for protein digestion is obtained from

   A. food B. air C. gastric juice D. none of these

2. The protein digesting juice is not digesting the stomach wall which is mainly made up of protein. The reason is

   A. due to some inactivity of the protein digesting juice to the protein of the stomach wall.

   B. an obstacle prevents to have contact with the protein of stomach.

   C. the protein digesting juice has the ability to digest only the protein in the food and not any other proteins.

D. the protein of the stomach wall is so powerful that protein digesting juice can not digest it.

E. none of these.

3. The shortage of secretion cause of the following ulcer

A. mucous B. HCl in the stomach

C. enzymes in the gastric juice. D. pepsin of the gastric juice

E. none of these

4. When we are with high emotions, change in the rate of digestion will

A. remain same B. increase C. decrease

D. depend on the nature of emotions

E. neither increase nor decrease

Usually a comet has two parts, a head and a very long shining tail. Central part of the head has more density and it looks like a small star and is called nucleus. The surrounding area of the nucleus is called coma. When a Dumakethu goes near the Sun, the substance from the head turns to the back and elongates into a tail. The tail will always be in the opposite direction to the Sun. Majority of the comets have only one tail. Rarely they have two tails and three tails. When it goes far away from the Sun the tail disappears. There are two reasons for the shining of the tail. First of all, it reflects light. Moreover, the powder substance in the tail has the ability to assimilate ultraviolet rays and emit visible light.

5. Comet and the Dhumakethu

A. are one and the same.

B. are the two different shapes of a single one.

6. The part of the comet which has greater density is

A. coma B. tail C. star

D. nucleus

7. When a comet approaches the sun from a long distance the comet's shape

A. will change B. will not change

C. changes sometimes

8. If we happened to see a comet in the sky in the east during the sun set, to which direction its tail will be

A. towards west B. towards east

C. towards south D. towards north

The moon which has 2160 mile diameter is only ¼ of the earth in size. It mass is only $\frac{1}{81}$ of that of earth. The gravitational force is proportional to the mass. The gravitational force of moon is $\frac{1}{6}$ of that of earth. These are some of the interesting results of them. A boy of 90 pounds weight will weigh only 15 pounds on the earth. A worker who carees a bag of rice can carry 6 bags of rice on the moon without any difficulty. A boy can also take his father on his shoulders and play without any difficulty.

We know that the stone which is thrown upwards returns to the earth because of the earth's gravitational force. Depending on the force with which we throw the stone rises up and returns. What must be the speed if we can throw a stone into space–25,000 miles per hour, i.e., 7 miles per second. Then only it can be free from the gravitational force. This speed can be called escape velocity. The spaceship can go away from earth only if it has this speed. But the escape velocity on moon is only 5,000 miles per hour—not even 1½ miles per second.

9. On the moon a boy can take his father on his shoulders because

   A. the weight of the boy decreases on the moon.

   B. the weight of the father decreases on the moon.

   C. since the moon is small in size.

10. How many kilograms can a boy lift on the earth if he can lift 120 kg. on the moon ?

    A. 20 kg. B. 120 kg. C. 720 kg.

11. The gravitational force of the moon is lesser than that of earch because

    A. the moon is far away from the earth

    B. the moon is smaller than the earth

    C. the moon has lesser mass than the earth

12. Two men of equal strength are throwing up stones–one man from the moon and the other from the earth. Then

    A. the man on the earth can raise the stone more

    B. the man on the moon can raise the stone more

    C. both of them can raise the stone to the same extent.

13. Two rockets of the same power are sent with the same speed, one from the earth to the moon and the other from the moon to the earth. Which rocket will land with more force ?

    A. both with the same force

    B. on the moon

    C. on the earth

The dreadful disease causing nature of pathogen depends on two important factors. They are, ability of pathogen to spread and multiply after entering the body as well as the poisionous substance called toxin which it produces. There are different types of pathogens based on the quantity of toxin they produce. In general, they produce two types of toxins. One type of highly poisionous and can cause diseases like Diphtheria. They emit exotoxins. Fortunately, the exotoxin that they produce is a protein, hence they are destroyed by heat and passage of time. There is another type called endotoxin. These will not be destroyed by heat and comparatively they are less poisionous. The micro-organisms that are responsible for digestive diseases produce mainly endotoxin.

First of all pathogen has to face the white blood cells. These are the blood cells that engulf and destroy the disease causing organisms that enter into the body. But on certain occasions the body may not withstand the very rapidly increasing pathogen. On such situations the body depends on a special resistance—the production of protein called antibody.

14. Pathogens are dreadful organisms primarily because

    A. they have the ability to multiply.

    B. they have the ability to enter the body.

    C. they have the ability to multiply and emit poison.

15. The pathogen that enters into the body has to face at first

    A. the white blood cells (phagocytes) of the blood

    B. the red blood cells of the blood

    C. none of the above.

16. One of the important characteristics of protein is

    A. do good to us always. B. not resisting the heat.

    C. do bad to us. D. the long existence.

THANK YOU YOUNG FRIEND

SCORING KEY

KERALA UNIVERSITY SCIENCE APTITUDE TEST

Test 1 Number Series

	A	B	C	D	E
1	⊕	O	O	O	O
2	O	O	O	O	⊕
3	O	O	O	⊕	O
4	O	⊕	O	O	O
5	O	O	⊕	O	O
6	O	O	⊕	O	O
7	⊕	O	O	O	O
8	⊕	O	O	O	O
9	O	O	⊕	O	O
10	O	O	O	O	⊕
11	O	O	O	O	⊕
12	O	O	O	⊕	O
13	O	O	O	O	⊕
14	O	O	⊕	O	O
15	O	⊕	O	O	O
16	O	O	⊕	O	O
17	O	O	O	⊕	O
18	O	⊕	O	O	O
19	⊕	O	O	O	O
20	⊕	O	O	O	O
21	⊕	O	O	O	O
22	O	O	O	⊕	O
23	⊕	O	O	O	O
24	⊕	O	O	O	O

Test 2 Science Information

	T	F		T	F
1	O	⊕	11	O	⊕
2	⊕	O	12	O	⊕
3	O	⊕	13	⊕	O
4	O	⊕	14	O	⊕
5	⊕	O	15	O	⊕
6	⊕	O	16	⊕	O
7	⊕	O	17	O	⊕
8	O	⊕	18	⊕	O
9	⊕	O	19	O	⊕
10	⊕	O	20	O	⊕

Test of 3 Formulation

	A	B	C	D	E
1	O	O	O	⊕	O
2	O	⊕	O	O	O
3	O	O	O	⊕	O
4	O	O	O	⊕	O
5	O	O	O	⊕	O
6	O	O	O	O	⊕
7	O	⊕	O	O	O
8	O	O	⊕	O	O
9	O	O	⊕	O	O
10	O	⊕	O	O	O

Test 4 Spatial Ability

	A	B	C	D	E	F
1	O	O	⊕	⊕	O	O
2	⊕	O	⊕	O	O	O
3	⊕	O	O	⊕	O	O
4	⊕	⊕	O	O	O	O
5	O	⊕	⊕	O	O	⊕
6	⊕	⊕	O	O	⊕	O
7	O	O	⊕	O	O	⊕
8	⊕	⊕	O	O	O	O
9	O	O	O	⊕	O	⊕
10	O	⊕	O	⊕	O	⊕
11	O	O	O	⊕	⊕	⊕
12	O	⊕	O	⊕	⊕	O
13	⊕	O	⊕	O	⊕	O
14	⊕	⊕	O	O	O	⊕
15	⊕	⊕	O	⊕	O	O
16	⊕	⊕	⊕	O	O	O
17	⊕	⊕	O	O	⊕	O
18	⊕	⊕	⊕	O	O	O
19	⊕	O	O	⊕	⊕	O
20	O	O	⊕	O	⊕	⊕

Test 5 Verbal Comprehension & Interpretation

	A	B	C	D	E
1	O	O	O	⊕	O
2	O	⊕	O	O	O
3	⊕	O	O	O	O
4	O	O	⊕	O	O
5	O	⊕	O	O	O
6	O	O	O	⊕	O
7	⊕	O	O	O	O
8	O	⊕	O	O	O
9	O	⊕	O	O	O
10	⊕	O	O	O	O
11	O	O	⊕	O	O
12	O	⊕	O	O	O
13	O	⊕	O	O	O
14	O	O	⊕	O	O
15	⊕	O	O	O	O
16	O	⊕	O	O	O

SCORES

Test 1______

Test 2______

Test 3______

Test 4______

Test 5______

Total ☐

Index